S. L. McKinlay

A widely admired swing.

Editor of the Glasgow Evening Times *and golf columnist for the Glasgow* Herald.

The four semi-finalists in the 1947 British Amateur championship at Carnoustie: (from left) S. L. McKinlay, W. Turnesa, R. Chapman, J. Campbell.

THE CLASSICS OF GOLF

Original Edition of

SCOTTISH GOLF AND GOLFERS

A COLLECTION OF WEEKLY GOLF COLUMNS FROM THE GLASGOW HERALD 1956–1980

by

S. L. McKinlay

Foreword by Herbert Warren Wind
Publisher's Note by Robert Macdonald
Afterword by K. M. Cameron

To Marian
who, though a non-golfer, shared with me
so many of my Scottish golfing experiences.

Permission to reprint "Golf and Golfers" columns from the Glasgow
Herald in book form from the Glasgow *Herald* and George Outram
& Co. Copyright, the Glasgow *Herald* and George Outram & Co.
Reprinted by Ailsa Inc., 1992.
ISBN 0-940889-37-4.

Foreword

This book—a collection of seventy-three of the winter-season-only weekly Tuesday columns called "Golf and Golfers" that Sam McKinlay, the widely admired Scottish editor, writer, and golfer, provided for the Glasgow Herald *from 1956 through 1980—was the idea of Robert Macdonald, the publisher of The Classics of Golf. Macdonald, among his other talents, has a nice creative mind. For example, since there was no definitive book about Harry Vardon, the first great modern golfer, he came up with the idea of creating such a book by putting together parts of four books that Vardon had written with four different journalists during his lengthy career. A fervent admirer of Bernard Darwin's work, Macdonald later found the time to read through his voluminous output and to produce for the Classics "The Darwin Sketchbook", a collection of Darwin's portraits of the outstanding champions and other top golfers he had watched in action from 1900 to 1955 and, in addition, knew well off the course.*

As an old friend of Sam McKinlay's—we met in 1950— I wrote to him when The Classics of Golf was getting started in the early 1980s and asked him if there were any relatively unknown golf books he thought we should consider for our series of quality reprints. Sam strongly recommended "A History of Golf" by Robert Browning, a Scottish golf scholar and journalist who had been based in London most of his life as the editor of Golfing *magazine. Sam considered "A History of Golf", which had been published in Great Britain and the United States in 1955, to be far and away the best one-volume history of the game. In any event, we settled on it as the fifth selection of The Classics of Golf. We asked Sam to provide the After-*

word. He sent us a beauty. Somewhat later—I think it was in the Classics' third year—when we were going down the stretch with our Vardon volume, Robert got in touch with Sam and asked him if he might be able to supply the Afterword. A few weeks later, he received another absolute gem from Sam. It so happened that back in 1919, when Sam was eleven, he had, at his father's suggestion, journeyed by street-car from the east end of the city, where the family lived, to the Killermont course of the Glasgow Golf Club in the west end of the city to watch the Victory Tournament, a match-play event that had been organized to celebrate the end of the First World War. All the best golfers were there from the Great Triumvirate (Vardon, J.H. Taylor, and James Braid) to the rising young stars like George Duncan and Abe Mitchell. It was Vardon who mesmerized young McKinlay and became his first golf hero.

It should be noted, in passing, that from the outset The Classics of Golf has paid only a modest fee to some of the best minds in the game to write the Afterwords for its selections. They have produced a succession of brilliant pieces.

I don't remember just when it was—it may have been in late September, 1988, shortly after "Vardon on Golf" had been sent to the printers—that Macdonald and McKinlay met each other. That autumn, Robert and a group of his golfing friends had flown to Britain for a ten-day golf holiday. As is usual on such expeditions, they played thirty-six holes a day, visiting a number of the historic championship courses along with a few uncelebrated ones which suited their itinerary. Before heading home, Robert had a good visit with Sam. Only a short time before this, the McKinlays had decided to give up their home in Bearsden in the west end of Glasgow. Sam's wife Marian had been worn down by the harsh Scottish winters, and, on the advice of her doctors, the McKinlays moved to the milder climate of southern England. They settled in Woking, a town some thirty miles southwest of London, in which their one child, Margaret (called Paddy), lived with her husband and two children. Sam had been retired for some time by then and would soon be edging into his eighties, but his hair was still brown, his skin pink, and his mind as keen as ever. Robert and Sam very much enjoyed each other's company. One year later, they got together again in Woking. I forget whether they had any business to transact, but it proved to be a fruitful visit. Robert was interested in finding out all he could about the golf columns that Sam had written for the Glasgow Herald, *and, with Sam's assistance, he got in touch with the right men at the George Outram company, the longtime owners and publishers of the Glasgow* Herald *and the* Evening Times. *They gave The Classics of Golf permission to reproduce a selection of columns and suggested that any compensation be directed to Sam. Fortunately, Sam had dutifully saved all three hundred and forty-five of his columns. He handed them over to Robert.*

During the past two years, the project gradually began to take shape. Robert read through the columns and arrived at a basic format. He got in touch with Kenneth Cameron, a prominent resident of Nairn and McKinlay's closest friend over the years, and he prevailed on him to write something about Sam. It proved to be a splendid piece, not quite as informal as K. M. Cameron really is. Thirteen times the Amateur champion of Nairnshire, he is such a helplessly exuberant fellow that after he has broken par on a round at Nairn, or anywhere else, he usually telephones Sam that night and takes at least forty-five minutes to describe the shimmering stroke-by-stroke beauty of his round. K. M. Cameron's reminiscence appears as the Afterword.

This past winter, after checking with Robert, McKinlay asked his old friend and associate Percy Huggins to send a letter to The Classics of Golf. From his many years of working with Percy, Sam knew that he would get the facts right about his newspaper career. Percy was the golf writer for the Glasgow Evening Times *for decades, and, after that, the editor of Britain's best monthly golf magazine. The two longtime friends have many things in common. They have always looked twenty years younger than their age, for example, and tough deadlines held no dread for them. In his letter to Robert, Percy wrote, "Hope this meets requirements. There is so much more I could have said." His note goes like this:*

"When, in 1936, I began reporting golf events for an evening paper in Glasgow, Scotland, Sam McKinlay (or "S.L." as he was known) was already well-established in golfing circles both as a player and as a writer. Scotland, in the early '30s, overflowed with amateur golfers of outstanding ability, but Sam had been good enough to have played for Scotland in six of the preceding seven years; he was to do so three times more. Additionally, he had been a member of the home team that played the United States in the 1934 Walker Cup match at St. Andrews, so his status as a golfer was established outside, as well as inside, Scotland.

"An honors graduate of Glasgow University, he joined the editorial staff of the Glasgow Herald *and became a distinguished leader writer. As an extra, he contributed a weekly column to a sister picture publication, the* Bulletin. *In those days amateurs of distinction could not write about golf under their own names, so Sam did so as "Our Golf Correspondent". However, virtually everyone in golf in Scotland knew who that correspondent was, and his columns were compulsory reading. They also had a considerable influence on the game in Scotland.

"The Second World War interrupted those writings and also robbed Sam of what might have been his best competitive years. They resumed after hostilities ended and continued until the Bulletin, *like other picture publications, suc-cumbed to the onset of TV. Subsequently, and for many years, his articles continued in the Glasgow* Herald.

"*In 1947, when he was in his 40th year, Sam came up with one of his many fine playing achievements when he reached the semi-finals of the (British) Amateur champion-ship (won by Willie Turnesa of the U.S). That performance gained him yet another appearance in a Scottish team.*

"*Thereafter serious competitive golf seemed to take sec-ond place as he concentrated on a career that took him, in the 1950s, to the editorship of the evening paper for which I worked. We had, I think, a happy relationship. On the golf side he was a distinguished member of the Royal and An-cient Golf Club of St. Andrews, and he served as a Walker Cup team selector and as a Rules of Golf committeeman.*

"*Sam McKinlay was a purist, and still is, both in golf and in his writings. As a player he had a swing that was widely admired and, indeed, envied. It was a swing in the classic mould, as were his writings. He had a great love of the English language, and woe betide the staff man who used a comma when it should have been a semi-colon. As a golf writer he ranked, in Britain, alongside Bernard Darwin and Henry Longhurst, and, in the United States, Grantland Rice and the inimitable Herb Graffis.*

"*It is only fitting that the best of his writings should be given a wider audience and preserved for posterity in book form.*"

I might have heard of Sam McKinlay earlier, but I re-ally did not become positively aware of him until shortly after the Second World War. I was researching a book on golf and was reminded that in 1934 the British Walker Cup team was captained by the Honorable Michael Scott who, the previous year, had won the British Amateur at the record age of fifty-five. On the first day of that match, which was held at St. Andrews, four 36-hole Scotch four-somes were played, as is traditional. (In foursomes the two partners play alternate shots and drive from alternate tees.) The team of Scott and McKinlay—Sam was half his partner's age—lost a close match against H. Chandler Egan and Max Marston, 3 and 2. In the singles the second day, Scott, playing at the top of the order against Johnny Goodman, the winner of the 1933 United States Open, went down 7 and 6 in their 36-hole match. McKinlay also lost his singles, 3 and 1, after a well-played match with Gus Moreland, a gifted young Texan. In 1947, McKinlay at forty was back in the news again. He entered the British Amateur during his brief summer vacation, as usual. At Carnoustie, he surprised everyone by going all the way to the semi-finals. There he lost to Dick Chapman, the American star, 2 down on the eighteenth green. (Willie Turnesa defeated Chapman in an all-American final.)

I met Sam three years later when the British Amateur was played at St. Andrews. By that time I had read some articles of his in British golf magazines. We met in a memorable way. One day around noon I was entering the crowded Big Room of the R. and A. clubhouse by the interior rear door when I bumped into Sam, whom I knew by sight. (I had watched him play some holes.) I introduced myself to him. We had been chatting for a couple of minutes when Bernard Darwin slowly eased his way into the room through the rear door. He had a cheery hello for Sam and, after turning and greeting me, he said to us with an approving smile before making his way through the mob to his leather armchair at the other end of the Big Room, "I see you have met each other."

Sam and I got together at fairly frequent intervals after that. He was on hand for the 1953 Walker Cup match at the Kittansett Club, in Marion, Massachusetts. I made it a point to get together with Sam whenever I went over to cover a Walker Cup match, a British Amateur, or a British Open that was held in Scotland. In 1955, for instance, Sam and Marian entertained me in Glasgow after the

Walker Cup match at St. Andrews. Sam had work to do at the paper, but he arranged for me to play my first rounds at Prestwick and Troon. He got over to the States in the late 1950s and the early 1960s to take in the Masters. An earnest bird-watcher, he was transported at Augusta by the song of the mockingbird. He admired the inventive design of the Augusta National. He loved being out on the rolling course on a brilliantly sunny April day watching Palmer, urged on by his Army, come charging down the second nine, undeterred by the wind or weather from attempting to carry with a daring second shot the water hazards guarding the green on the two short par 5s, the thirteenth and the fifteenth, and thereby setting himself up for a crack at an eagle or at least a birdie that could vault him into the lead. Visitors from Britain adore the Masters, but Sam is the only one I have heard say, "We should build long holes like these, with strategic water hazards, in Britain. The leader isn't safely home until he gets by them, and his pursuers still have a chance to catch him if they can rise to the occasion."

Samuel Livingstone McKinlay was one of the five children of John and Anne Campbell Neill McKinlay, both of whom were born in Glasgow. Mr. McKinlay was what was called in his day a commercial traveller, and is known today as a travelling representative or a rep, for the Glasgow firm of Ritchie and Osborne. Two weeks each month he travelled to Dundee and the neighboring cities and towns on the East coast selling butter, eggs, ham, cheese, and allied provisions, and the other two weeks he travelled to Fort William, Oban, and other towns on the West coast. In those days he travelled almost exclusively by train, as most commercial travellers did. He was a splendid card player, especially celebrated for his skill at a game called solo whist.

Four of the five children of John and Anne McKinlay

were boys. The oldest, David, retired from British Petroleum (or BP) some years ago. He served as deputy general manager of the Abadan Refinery at the head of the Persian Gulf until the Iranians confiscated it. (When he returned to Britain, he became a fuel economist at BP's main office.) Next in line was Anne, who died a few years ago. Then came Sam. He was born in 1907. He was followed some five years later by John, Jr., who was called Jack, and, finally, by Neill. All four sons eventually played to single-figure handicaps. Indeed, on a Saturday in late spring a good many years ago, Dave brought in the low round at Royal Wimbledon's spring meeting, Jack brought in the low round at Prestwick St. Nicholas, and Sam did the same at Killermont. Mr. McKinlay never played to anything lower than a four handicap, but he adored the game.

Sam first broke 100 with a round of 95 as a junior member of the Alexandra Club's Lethamhill course in the East End of Glasgow. At eighteen he set a new course record at Lethamhill with a 68 in a team stroke competition. "I had my photo in the Evening Times *the next day and thought I was Scotland's answer to Bobby Jones," he wrote me not long ago in recalling his early years in golf. Sam took his first golf lesson on his sixteenth birthday. His father bought him a driver and a brassie made by David Adams, a noted Glasgow clubmaker, and Mr. Adams threw in a five-minute lesson. Sam took his next lesson from Gregor McIntosh, the professional at Nairn— his present to himself on his fiftieth birthday.*

I received some of the previous information from Sam earlier this year. With the publication date of "Scottish Golf and Golfers" drawing close, I wrote to him and asked him to answer a long list of questions. (We have corresponded for decades, exchanging four or five long letters a year.) He answered the queries carefully, as is his wont. Unquestionably, the best method to deal with the infor-

mation Sam provided is to quote from sections of his letter:

On his best golf: "I never won any tournaments of real consequence, but I was a useful performer in one-day, 36-hole tournaments in the West of Scotland. I won most of the 'big' ones, the prestige ones with several internationalists in the field. My best win, I suppose, was at Glasgow Gailes in 1933 in the Edward Trophy when I did 70,66—no one had ever scored so low in such a competition. Oddly, my 66 had a 7 in it at the tenth hole after I had gone out in 30, six under par. That 66 was my lowest score in a competition. My lowest ever was a 63 at Crow Wood in mid-winter, seven under par including two penalty strokes. Just one of those days when I holed everything."

On his years at Glasgow University: "I was there from 1925 to 1929. I took a first in English Language and Literature. I don't remember being impressed especially by any books apart from Robert Browning's poems, and that was largely after hearing Sybil Thorndike, a good actress who was the first St. Joan in Shaw's play, speaking verse at the Students Union. It was an unforgettable experience—the hall crammed to the rafters, every word audible, all the verses from memory. I, of course, had to read very widely at University, but it was really more like work than the kind of pleasure I now get out of reading."

On his work as a newspaperman: "My first job was as a junior sub-editor on the Glasgow Herald. I think that the American equivalent of sub-editor is re-write man. A sub prepared raw copy for the printer. He cut it to size, corrected the grammar and other things, marked which type should be used, wrote the headings. It could be dreary when you were subbing, say, agricultural reports and long lists of cattle prices, but it could be wonderfully exciting and demanding when you had to handle, say, a Parliamentary occasion, a foreign story such as the murder of Dr. Dollfuss, the Austrian Chancellor , or any big news story. I joined the paper on Armistice Day, 1929, and Outram & Co. were my only employer until I retired in 1971. I graduated from the subs to the leader (or editorial) writers staff in 1937 and was a general leader writer covering every sort of subject until I became editor of the Evening Times in 1953. The Herald and Times in my day were broadly conservative but they took a very firm line on Munich, so firm that some industrialists like Sir James Lithgow, a prominent shipbuilder, threatened to take away their advertising. There certainly was no slavish following of the Conservative party line. I remember approving a very sharp Times editorial after Alec Douglas Home said he had "lived among miners" all his life—just because there was a pit about six miles from his Lanarkshire home. I lived only a few miles from Clydebank but would never have claimed to live among shipyard workers.

"The Times certainly had a large working-class readership, but it was also a badge of respectability for the city business and professional men. Glasgow had at one time six first-division soccer-football teams. There are four now but only two really matter, Celtic and Rangers. They're known as the Old Firm, and their clashes are in a class by themselves for passion, partisanship, and, at times, sectarian friction, Celtic being largely Roman Catholic, Rangers rootedly opposed to Roman Catholicism, though a few years ago they did sign a Catholic, Mo Johnson, who used to play for Celtic. That was a front-page story in virtually every newspaper in Britain.

"My working week on the Herald was five days, or rather evenings. On the Times I worked an 11-day fortnight, taking every second Saturday off. I can't remember what holidays I had on the Herald, but I usually managed a week off to play in the Amateur championship. I played in it every year from 1928 until the early 1950s. I *did not play that regularly in the Scottish Amateur championship but I played often enough, and well enough, to be selected for the Scottish international team most years from 1929 until 1947. My game had no special merit except that I think I was pretty good from about 130 yards in. I was influenced by lots of players. George Duncan was an early hero, and so was Henry Cotton. I admired Cotton so much that I once spent weeks perfecting his method. At the end of this period I met an old friend whom I had not seen for some time. "Ah," he said, 'I see you've got the same old swing'. Exit Cotton."*

Sam became a member of the Royal and Ancient Golf Club of St. Andrews in 1951. He served several three-year terms on the Rules of Golf Committee and also served on the Ball and Implements Committee. No one in the club impressed him more than Stewart Lawson, a chartered accountant who was a member of a distinguished St. Andrews family. Over a very long period—say, five decades— Stewart understood the rules of golf better than any other member of the R. and A. Before Sam joined the club, he had corresponded with Bernard Darwin. One of Darwin's passionate interests was famous British murders. During the war Sam sent him a book on that subject by W. N. Roughhead, an Edinburgh lawyer, which had earned a rave review in the Glasgow Herald. Along with being a connoisseur of murder and murderers, Roughhead was also a director of the Edinburgh Crematorium Society. On learning about this, Darwin wrote in a letter to Sam, "It is a pleasing thought that Roughhead is the director of an establishment that offers murderers the best means of disposing of the proceeds of their industry."

Sam did not get to meet Bobby Jones until 1946. That year he made his first trip to the United States, traveling here on the Queen Elizabeth's maiden voyage. When he visited Atlanta, Charlie Yates took him out to the East

*Lake Golf Club to meet Jones. Bob had previously ar-
ranged to play with some old friends that day, a Saturday. "Bob invited me to play with him on the Tuesday, but
I had to fly back to New York to make the return trip on
the* Queen Elizabeth," *Sam remembers clearly. "I missed
the chance of a lifetime. That was probably the greatest
disappointment in my golfing life. The best-known golfers
I played with were Walter Hagen and Horton Smith. They
had come over to Britain as members of American Ryder
Cup teams which found the time to play a tune-up match
against a team of Scottish amateurs at Whitecraigs, a
course on the south side of Glasgow. I had a close game
with Horton Smith in 1929. Four years later I beat Hagen
by a couple of strokes—quite the most enjoyable round I
have ever played with anyone. He was generous with his
praise, the perfect opponent, and great fun.*

*"My golf swing just grew, without too much conscious
thought on my part. I don't know that I learned anything
specifically from studying Vardon, Hagen, and Duncan,
except that they made a picture in my mind of true elegance. Jones was different. I saw him play in our Open at
St. Andrews in 1927, and from the first I retained a picture of grace and elegance, and power, too. It was inde-
finable but inescapable. Another golfer who influenced
me was Gene Sarazen. To be precise, four photographs of
Sarazen did. They showed him playing a long pitch with
what used to be called a mashie-niblick. The photos appeared on four consecutive pages of* Golf Monthly *sometime in the Twenties: address, top of the backswing; impact; and follow-through. I learned more from those
photos than from anything else or anyone else. Gene was,
of course, a wonderful man as well as one of the truly
great players."*

*I had known Sam a dozen years or so before I had the
pleasure of playing golf with him. In early 1963, knowing
that I would have a week or ten days free after covering*

the Walker Cup match in late May at the Turnberry course on the West coast of Scotland, I wrote to Sam and asked him if he might be able to arrange to take a week off from his work so that we could travel to one of the famous old Scottish courses that was situated far off the Glasgow-Edinburgh sector where visiting foreign golfers cluster in the summer months. At that time, I was still on the sunny side of fifty, but my golf had become very erratic. If I broke eighty on a fairly good course, it was a big day for me. Sam was then in his middle fifties, but he looked much younger than his age. He had always taken good care of himself, and, at five-feet nine, he had kept his weight at around a hundred and sixty pounds. He was a fine-looking man with that eminently Scottish combination of strong features, blue eyes, pink cheeks, and light brown hair with a touch of marmalade in it. His youthful appearance was hard on Marian. She was a pretty woman with a trim figure, but her hair had turned gray-white prematurely. "I had an interesting conversation the other day," she told me on our trip. "I was out walking when a lady who had recently moved into our neighborhood came over and introduced herself. She said that she had seen me out walking with my son several times." Marian is the daughter of a doctor, a general practitioner from Banff-shire who moved to Glasgow in 1912 to join the school medical service in Stirlingshire. Marian and Sam met at Millport, a holiday resort on the Clyde, in 1929, after Sam had finished his final exams at Glasgow University. They were married in 1936. After graduating from high school, Marian had no inclination to go on to a university, and she trained instead as a hairdresser and beautician in a plush establishment in Glasgow. One of Marian and Sam's great enthusiasms has been bird-watching. Both of them are very fond of Muriel Spark's books and articles because she describes the kind of middle-class life in Edinburgh that they knew in Glasgow. Marian never learned to play golf, but she knows the game well, and, like many Scottish women who aren't golfers, she has learned to be a capable putter and can be a fearsome opponent on the nine- and eighteen-hole putting greens that have long been a standard facility at the top resort hotels in Scotland. Sam recently said of Marian, "She has always been interested, in a sort of detached way that was helpful, in my golf, and she has always been an awfully good judge of my writing, for she has an instinctive feeling for any lapse of taste." A word about their daughter Margaret, whom they call Paddy. She trained as a teacher and taught in a primary school before marrying John MacIsaac, a mechanical engineer, who is a shipping economist for Shell International Marine. They have two sons in their twenties. Kenneth, the elder, is a mechanical engineer. Donald is in business management. Their grandfather taught them how to play golf.

Back to the late spring of 1963 and my golf trip with the McKinlays. The day after the conclusion of the Walker Cup match, we headed north into the Highlands, Sam at the wheel. Our destination was the town of Dornoch in the northeast corner of Scotland. Long an admirer of the course of the Royal Dornoch Golf Club, Sam felt that it was important that I should see it. (At that time, only a handful of Americans were aware of Dornoch. Today the course is so popular that the club cannot take care of all the touring Americans who want to play it.) As we were nearing Inverness, the capital city of the Highlands, late in the afternoon, we broke our drive north by peeling off to the east where we spent three days in Nairn, a summer resort long favored by discerning folks like Harold Macmillan. Nairn sits on the southern bank of the lovely Moray Firth. On a clear day you can see the glistening mountain peaks on the west coast of Ross and Cromarty some fifty or sixty miles away. As was noted earlier, Nairn is the home of the McKinlays' close friends, Kenny and Mar-

garet Cameron. I played three rounds with Kenny and Sam on the rather testing course of the Nairn Golf Club. A cold and rather stiff wind was blowing down from the north, and I spent a good deal of time hacking my way out of the prickly gorse bushes in the heavy rough. Kenny and Sam were able to handle the wind, and they brought in beautiful rounds in the low 70s.

Dornoch in those days was a drive of slightly over four hours from Inverness, for at that time the principal roads to the far north were narrow and twisting. We drove into a glorious burst of summer weather that warmed and gilded all of Britain for ten straight days. This was a wonderful piece of luck, for Dornoch is situated at 58° North Latitude, the same as Juneau, Alaska. The county seat of Sutherland, it is a neat and charming resort town which, at the time of our visit, had a permanent population of under a thousand. Its lovely cathedral is built of mellowed yellow sandstone, as are most of the town's other buildings. The links of Dornoch, only a few hundred yards from the main square, are perched well above the North Sea. At the time of our visit the small two-story clubhouse, save for the installation of a new bar, must have been the same as it had been in 1904 when the club celebrated the official opening of its extended eighteen holes. Golf was played in Dornoch as early as 1616, which makes the course the third oldest in the world. (St. Andrews and Leith antedated it.) Like St. Andrews, Dornoch is a loop-type course. Eight outward holes were built along a high shelf of land that tumbles in various ways. The terrain keeps changing, as does the swing and direction of the fairways, the bunkering, and the siting of the greens. As a result, each hole has its own distinct personality. The same applies to the ten incoming holes which ramble up and down the crusty higher land and the gentler duneland by the sea. The greens are not flattish continuations of the fairways as they are on many early Scot-

tish courses. They rise somewhat abruptly two feet or more above the fairway. They are fast and delicately contoured. Dornoch survived as a popular golf resort down through the last hundred years for several reasons. One important one was that golf-oriented, well-to-do English families, like the Holdernesses and the Wethereds, annually spent their summers there.

On the day Sam and I played Dornoch, a swirling wind was abroad. For whatever reason, we were the only players on the course. Sam dragged his clubs behind him on his trolley. He always carried it in the luggage compartment of his car, along with his clubs and his spiked shoes. He never took a caddie. The club professional kindly got hold of his ten-year-old grandson to caddy for me. We strapped my heavy American bag to a trolley, and the boy handled it with no trouble. Sam was around in 72 without making a putt of any length. He made it look easy. I don't believe he was ever in the rough. I started off fairly well and then, picking up the tempo of Sam's swing, played some real good stuff the rest of the way. I even holed a few putts. Sam was delighted.

The next day was a Sunday. Royal Dornoch was closed. So was just about everything else in northern Scotland. The people in that part of the country are strict observers of the Sabbath. We drove to the west coast for lunch on a two-lane highway that frequently narrowed to one lane, and then we drove back to Dornoch. I had been looking forward to playing Royal Dornoch on Monday, but Sam would not let me. He wanted to be sure I went home with fond memories of the course. In the morning we played the eighteen-hole course in the nearby village of Golspie. How good a golfer is Sam McKinlay? Well, that morning he warmed up by swinging his 3-iron for about fifteen seconds to get the feel of the shaft and the head. The first hole is a par 3 of about 170 yards. Sam put his tee-shot five feet from the hole. Without sinking anything much, he was around in 68. I played very few good shots. I was fortunate we hadn't played Dornoch again. That afternoon Sam permitted me to walk Dornoch. We rambled over it together, breathing in the singular qualities which in recent years have made it such a magnet for golfers from around the world and such an inspiriting test of a person's ability to play golf shots.

I think I should mention two brief incidents which took place on our trip, for they reveal, I think, an important part of Sam McKinlay's character. On the first day, as we were driving east from Glasgow across the central Lowlands as we headed for the highway that would take us north into the Highlands via Pitlochry, Sam took a short cut he knew that would get us out of the fairly heavy traffic and directly to the route we wanted. It was a strange road made of thick, heavy sand. It was hardly wider than the width of a car and was hemmed in on both sides by fairly tall and very thick scrubby bushes and strange stunted trees. I was sitting in the back seat, and, since the ashtray was filled with cigarette butts—in those days nearly all of us were heavy smokers—I mentioned to Sam that this looked like a good place to dump the backseat ashtray. There was a momentary silence and then Sam said in a somewhat frosty voice, "We don't do that here, Herb". Sam is at all times a law-respecting Scot. He believes that laws exist to maintain order and to protect the quality of life, and that it is everyone's duty to respect the law, stated or implicit. When we stopped for gas an hour later at a gas station on the highway, we dumped the ashtrays into a proper receptacle. Sam admires and respects his country and Scottish traditions. Later in our trip, after our pleasant stay in Nairn, there was a brief incident on the way to Inverness and the north that I wasn't prepared for. Culloden Moor, where in 1746 British troops under the command of the Duke of Cumberland routed the Jacobite army that supported the cause of

Prince Charles Edward, "Bonnie Prince Charlie", lay just off the road on which we were traveling. Sam thought that I might like to see the historic battlefield. There weren't many visitors that day, and we were able to park at the side of the road adjacent to Culloden Moor. As I got out of the car, I found myself looking up at a large, impressive monument, but I couldn't immediately make out who or what it commemorated. It probably marked a hero's grave, I surmised. I took my cap off and started to search for some description of of the memorial. "Put your cap back on," Sam said sharply. "That's not the tomb of a great man. It's just a monument to Cumberland. He was nothing but a butcher." All of us looked out over Culloden Moor for a moment or two. Then we got back in the car and continued on our way.

I think you will enjoy getting to know Sam McKinlay.

Herbert Warren Wind

TABLE OF CONTENTS

PART I

THE FIRST COLUMN
(OCTOBER 17, 1956)

PART II

PEOPLE

PART III

PLACES

PART IV

THINGS

PART V

THE LAST COLUMN
(MARCH 15, 1980)

SCOTTISH
GOLF
AND
GOLFERS

PART I

THE FIRST COLUMN
(*OCTOBER 17, 1956*)

The Lure of Length (1956)

"I suddenly within a week was exalted from being a short driver into a really long one." *James Braid*.

"I have been a good driver. My supporters would go even further and claim that I have driven straighter than possibly anyone in my generation." *Henry Cotton*.

"A woman is only a woman, but a hefty drive is a slosh." *P. G. Wodehouse*.

There is a fourth quotation which might be added to the three at the head of these reflections, but it is one that is the last refuge of short hitters, of the envious, of the puny, and of those whose only pride in golf is in their sly short game: "They don't pay off on the drive."

It is, of course, true that the smiter is not necessarily an accomplished golfer any more than the cricketer who delights in knocking the ball out of the ground is a reliable batsman. But the modern golf ball and modern implements, especially the modern iron club with its steel shaft and compact head, combine to diminish the rigours of recovery.

The long hitter in modern golf is more likely than his ancestor to "get away with it" and, as a result, there has grown up a race of long hitters. There is no doubt that the golfing gallery likes the long hitter and always has. Freddie Tait was beloved of the crowds because he kept them in delicious uncertainty as to when he would hit a vastly crooked tee-shot into some part of a course seen hitherto only by the greenkeeper or small boys seeking lost balls. And of Edward Blackwell it was once well said: "I doubt if any game has ever produced a more truly awesome spectacle than that of Mr. Edward Blackwell driving a golf ball—he was so palpably out for blood. He put everything he had into the stroke, even his eyebrows, and they were essentially formidable eyebrows."

Then there was the monumental Braid, hitting the ball "with divine fury," and the elegant Cyril Tolley, who once hit a drive on an Irish course so far off the line that his caddie, asked to "club" the next shot, shook his head and exclaimed, "The Lord ounly knows. No other blighter has ever been here before."

We cannot all be Taits and Tolleys, Braids or Blackwells, but which of us can lay hand on heart and avow that he does not cherish a long, straight drive above the brave putt or the rare iron shot hit like a shutting jackknife? Other things being equal, the long driver will always have the best of it.

What, then, is a long drive? We are short of standards in these days because the long-driving championship which used to be an accompaniment of the "Open" a generation ago has fallen into desuetude. There have been other tests, mainly of the amateurs' length, at odd times in recent years, and during the International week at Portmarnock in 1949 there was a long-driving competition which provided the Irishmen with a beanfeast— Bruen *carried* 280 yards, Carr 265 yards, and Carroll 250. None of the other countries could produce a player to get within 15 yards of Carroll.

They order things better in the United States. During this year's U.S. Open championship, held at Rochester, New York, the tenth series of driving tests was conducted during the actual play of the third round at the eighth hole. It was therefore a test, not a competition. There were no prizes, and if the players knew they were being tested, they were certainly of no mind to take risks with one drive merely to impress the officials of the U.S.G.A.

The collected results are of great interest and of some value, too. Conditions were good apart from the fact that after overnight rain the ground and air alike were heavy.

The fairway was 35 yards wide, it was marked every 10 yards from 200 to 300 yards from the tee, and a careful check was made on where the balls pitched and where they finished.

Of the 51 players tested, 33 hit the fairway—not, in my view, a very high proportion being, as they were, the cream of the crop. The average carry of the 33 was 239.63 yards, which was almost exactly the same as at previous tests conducted at the "Open" and therefore a fair indication that the ball manufacturers have been kept in control and the clubmakers have not been able to add much assistance despite their claims for their products.

The average of all the drives, including the run on the 33 balls that pitched on the fairway and also the wild ones, like Billy Joe Patton's, that were hooked outside the ropes, was 253.39 yards—which suggests that a fit James Bruen would stand the might of American golf on its ear if he could reproduce his Portmarnock form of seven years ago.

The longest ball of all was driven by one John Garrett, an amateur, whose tee-shot finished a foot in the rough 281 yards from the tee. De Vicenzo, whose booming tee-shots have made us catch our British breath, was right centre of the fairway one yard behind. Tommy Bolt, who is commonly more notable for the distance he throws clubs than for the distance he drives the ball, hit it 279 yards. Stranahan, Snead, and Middlecoff (the ultimate winner of the championship) were clustered plumb in the middle of the fairway nearly 270 yards out from the tee. Hogan was only a few yards behind and also, as we would expect, perfectly placed for his next shot.

One other statistic is enlightening. Of the drives that did not finish on the fairway, more were on the left than on the right. No fewer than nine balls were in a bunker just off the left edge of the fairway between the 230-yard and the 260-yard markers, and only one ball was in a bunker on the right between the 210-yard and the 230-yard markers. Of the 10 players so trapped, no fewer than seven reached the green with their second shots—a distance of 170 yards—which suggests great competence in their recovery play, uncommonly good luck in the lie, and accommodating low faces on the traps.

Of the crooked drives, the hooked ones went about five yards farther than the faded ones, proving once again what we all know, that the slice is the great consumer of distance. But the American tests prove something else: if you want to trap the tiger, set your trap on the left rather than on the right. Since the Americans "tailor" their courses before a championship and don't just accept what the host club can provide, no doubt even now they are planning penal hazards on the hooker's side of next year's course.

We are a good deal less precise in our thinking and planning, but I for one would like to see tests instituted on the American pattern at next year's Open championship. Muirfield would be a perfect course for such tests. The tenth fairway, as I recall, is fair and level and wide enough to beckon the drivers. If conditions were favourable we might learn a good deal to our advantage. The winner might even provide us with a comment to rival Braid's or Cotton's, though never Mr. Wodehouse's.

PART II

PEOPLE

The Fastest Golfer in the World (1957)

Two of the American golfers who will almost certainly play in this year's Ryder Cup match at Lindrick are distinguished for, among other things, the pace of their play. Cary Middlecoff, the holder of the American Open championship, is a monument of deliberation and has been known to take all of 20 minutes to play one hole. Doug Ford, on the other hand, is probably the fastest golfer in the world—certainly the fastest in the top echelons.

Middlecoff does not take an excessive time over the execution of his shots. In this respect he resembles Bobby Locke, who is a very fast player indeed once he has taken up his stance, although the preliminaries are protracted. Middlecoff is a brooder and a surveyor. He thinks nothing of walking 150 yards to spy out the terrain, and that means a return journey of the same distance, at a slow walking pace which his long legs do nothing to hasten. Back at the ball he stands and thinks for an unconscionable time before choosing his club, but, the choice once made, he does not waste time with waggles or the like.

Ford is different in every respect except that he, like Middlecoff and Locke, is a superb performer. Everything he does is at the double. I watched him play four holes at a Montreal course in a big-money tournament which he won narrowly—the last four holes, too, when the heat was on—and all that I clearly remember was his general attitude and his results.

How he achieved them I know not. He tees the ball, takes his stance, has the merest apology for a waggle, and then swings so fast that the unlucky onlooker who blinks misses everything. By the time the crowd's "Ooh" of ad-

miration has died away, Ford is 50 yards down the fairway and going like a man with the Indians after him.

If he has to wait for a moment to play his second shot,
he paces around like a caged tiger. Twice when I watched
him he hit a long second before the crowd in front had
cleared the green, twice he putted while his fellow-competitor was in the act of retrieving his ball from the hole,
and he knocked in his last putt of all—from 18 inches for
thousands of dollars—while the crowd's applause for the
excellence of his approach putt still hung on the air.

It is a pleasing thought that Ford might encounter in the
Ryder Cup match one of our sturdy veterans who is un-
hurried, calm, and methodical beyond the ordinary, Fred
Daly. Of Daly it might be said as was once said of Sandy
Herd: "The waggles are many but the shots are few." I
have seen Daly on the putting green lift his blade from
behind to over the ball (not in front as most golfers do) as
many as a dozen times before he finally makes up his
mind to make the stroke. But what a good putter he is! He
will never "miss 'em quick."

Speed on the links is largely a question of temperament,
although in America it is sometimes a question of temper-
ature. When the thermometer stands at 90 and humidity
is around the same mark, there is every reason for taking
one's time.

I play much faster now than I did 20 years ago, but then
I had the notion that a little more care would get me there.
It didn't, but for a long time I liked to think it would.

In making that error I was in good company, for many
golfers, some of the highest distinction, have chosen to
think that genius on the links, as in life, is an infinite
capacity for taking pains. All of us would do well to remember what a wiser man said about genius—that it is
mainly an affair of energy.

By that reckoning Ford, is a golfing genius, as were
George Duncan and Sarazen, two other players who

golfed at the gallop. When Sarazen played in the Open championship at St. Annes a few years ago, he was first man out in the first qualifying round and holed the course, if my memory serves, in under 70 and just over two hours.

Then there was the classic final in an Amateur championship at Muirfield in 1909 when Robert Maxwell beat C. K. Hutchison by one hole and the two rounds occupied only four hours, the golf being outstandingly good.

By contrast there was a match at Birkdale in the 1946 Amateur championship between Frank Stranahan and R. J. White in the fourth round at a time when all that was known of Stranahan was that he was very good, very rude, and very slow. White, not yet the famous player he became, decided to play him at the third part of Stranahan's game, and the match dragged its slow length along to the last green, which was reached in something over four hours, before White lost.

Mr. Darwin, commonly the kindest of critics, summed up the feelings of all who endured the dreary business with this sub-acid verdict: "Golf is not a funeral, though both can be very sad things."

"He Always Knew What To Do" (1958)

Few golfers of our time could live up to William Hazlitt's judgment on Cavanagh, the early nineteenth-century master of hand-fives, of whom the great essayist said: "He could do what he pleased, and he always knew what to do." One golfer who could was Henry Cotton. Another was Ben Hogan.

With his driver Cotton was very straight, and he was long into the bargain. At his best he drove better than any British professional has driven since Vardon. So severe a critic as the present chairman of the Walker Cup selectors was once heard to say of Cotton: "It is impossible to tell whether his drives are finishing on the right side or the left side of the fairway." What was true of his driving was equally true of his iron play—with this difference: when Cotton had to improvise he knew exactly what to do. At Carnoustie in 1937 I saw him play the best single shot I have ever seen any golfer play. It was at the ninth hole in the final round when the pressure was severe. He had hit a perfect drive and was ill-rewarded by finding the ball not only in a hanging lie but on a slope falling away from him.

It was the kind of stance and lie which insisted on a cut shot, but such a shot had virtually no hope of hitting and holding a green that was angled unfavourably for the player. The set of the green called for a shot with draw, the lie of the ball made a fade almost inevitable.

Cotton examined the position with his usual furrowed care, took a big iron, and miraculously, as it seemed to me, hit a perfect shot with a hint of draw right to the heart of the green. Cotton, clearly, could do what he pleased, because he knew what to do—and how to do it.

Hogan had something more; he knew what to do and how to do it—with every club in his bag. During his practice for the Open championship at Carnoustie, he set himself an unusual examination at the sixteenth hole, which is often a one-shotter but, in a head wind, is out of range of all but the leviathans of the links.

On Hogan's practice day the green was comfortably within reach of a wooden club and he played three balls, one with a driver, one with a brassie, the third with his spoon. All three balls finished within a few yards of the hole. Even the great Cavanagh would have doffed his cap to such virtuosity.

What was especially intriguing about Hogan's shot-making was that he could be seen to be thinking out the stroke. When he stood on the second tee at Carnoustie, for example, his slitty eyes could be seen focusing on the few yards of fairway between Braid's bunker and the rough on the left, because that is where a drive must be placed if the green is to lie open for the next shot. And down the narrow alley went Hogan's drive—not, if you please, a canny, steered shot but a full-blooded bang.

So he went round the great course. At the third hole, when I was watching him, he seemed much more concerned to survey the fourth fairway and the position of the pin on the distant green than with his approach shot to the tricky third. He knew what to do, and he could do it virtually at will.

Most of us may know what to do, but cannot do it because we lack the technical skill. Many of us do not even know what to do when there is a choice of shot. Hogan never seemed to be in any doubt, least of all at the last hole of all, where he hit an enormous drive when anything safe would have served. Hazlitt would have admired Hogan.

A Special Train for Snead (1962)

Sam Snead is now over 50 and therefore technically a senior golfer. He is eligible for the Teacher tournament, the supreme award of which is an expenses-paid trip to Britain to play the best British senior professional and also to compete in the Open championship.

The free trip might prove attractive, for Snead, in common with other highly paid American entertainers, makes a great parade of his parsimony; but a trip to Britain would appeal to him less than a hunting or fishing trip in the West Virginia mountains where he played his first bare-foot golf.

Snead has played golf in this country several times, never with enthusiasm though always with the great skill that has kept him in the top rank of professionals for almost 30 years. He tells some of the story, with a quite startling disregard for the truth, in a book which he has written in association with Al Stump, "The Education of a Golfer". The book, like Snead's golf, is first-class entertainment and also compact with excellent golfing advice; but it does little to improve the public image which Snead takes an almost perverse delight in exhibiting every time he sets tacket on turf.

He first came to these shores in 1937 when he was the youngest member of the U.S. Ryder Cup team. He won his international singles against Richard Burton, who was to win the Open championship at St. Andrews in 1939 and whom Snead was to succeed as holder of the title, also at St. Andrews, seven years later.

He had to be bullied by his sponsors into entering for the 1946 Open Championship. "It's time you won a big title overseas," he was told. "The prestige will be terrific."

To which Snead retorted, "What do I want with prestige? The British Open pays the winner $600 in American money. A man would have to be two hundred years old at that rate to retire from golf."

Anyway, Snead came, reluctantly, played magnificently, kept his head when all around him were losing theirs, and won comfortably by four strokes. But he did not enjoy the experience. "Along with Lawson Little," he said, "I rode a gully-jumper train up from London. We passed places with names like Kirkintilloch and the Firth of Forth and then we slowed down past some acreage that was so raggedy and beat-up that I was surprised to see what looked like a fairway amongst the weeds. Down home we wouldn't plant cow beets on land like that.

" 'Say, that looks like an old, abandoned golf course', I said to a man across the aisle, tapping his knee. 'What did they call it?'

"You'd have thought I stabbed him. 'My good sir!' he snorted, '*That* is the Royal and Ancient Golf Club of St. Andrews, founded in 1754! And it is not now, nor ever will be, abandoned!'

"He was so insulted, this Duke Something-or-Other, that the British papers made a fuss about my remark and from then on I was dodging reporters who had the knife out for me. The only place over there that is holier than St. Andrews is Westminster Abbey."

After that, according to Snead, "came caddie troubles. The way most golfers tell it, St. Andrews caddies are the world's best and can read the grass right down to the roots from Burn Hole, which is No. 1 to Home Hole. Mine were a bunch of bums. I had four caddies in four days. One of them whistled between his teeth when I putted. After letting him go I drew a fellow in sailor pants who couldn't judge distance or carry. On one hole he slipped me the 3-iron and said, 'That's the ticket, mate.' The shot left me 30 yards short of the green. The next hole he clubbed me with a 5-iron. This time I refused his advice, took a 7-iron, and even then landed over the green in a bunker. 'Mate, you're sunk,' I said, and gave him back to the caddie-master.''

Snead's next caddie, reputed to be St. Andrews' best, "went to jail for drunkenness the night before the Open started, leaving me to figure the course for myself."

"On No. 14, Hell's Bunker, a Scotsman stuck his whiskers in my face and said, 'You can shoot sixes from here on in, laddie, and win'." And to crown all, the alcoholic caddie "got himself sprung from jail and begged me to give him the winning ball. 'Maun,' he promised tearfully, 'I'll treasure it all my days.' An hour later he sold it for fifty quid, so he made more off the Open than I did."

Snead must have eaten a lot of turkey dinners, for no one has a better, sweeter, more rhythmic turn, and it's as smooth today as it was at Carnoustie in 1937 when first I saw him. If he does play as a senior, and qualifies for that free trip to Britain, I suggest that in penance he play at Kirkintilloch. Dr. Beeching will lay on a special train for him.

Lema without the Champagne (1964)

A friend of mine who numbers among his accomplishments an educated appreciation of the wine of our country was in the locker room of the Royal and Ancient clubhouse when Tony Lema arrived there after winning the Open championship in July.

A steward materialised with a tray and all the makings of what is usually known as a refreshment. The new champion was asked to name his potion, and before the wondering eyes of my friend and others he took the jug of water and drained it—and asked for more.

It is a simple tale, but a true one, and it is worth telling because Lema is widely held to be the playboy of the Western world of golf: Champagne Tony, because once in a moment of exuberance a little over two years ago, on the brink of his first success in a major tournament, he announced that if he won the sudden-death play-off with Bob Rosburg he would buy champagne for all who cared to share his triumph. He has since maintained this pleasing custom, though now at a sponsor's expense, and the press tent is a more cheerful place on that account.

Yet anyone who watched Lema at St. Andrews, both on the course and off it, must have found it difficult to reconcile the reputation with reality. There never was a more unflamboyant performer, one less given to eccentricities of speech and behaviour. His swing was beautiful to behold, his demeanour wholly admirable, and his performance, of course, was one of the great achievements in the golf of our time.

He landed at Prestwick about breakfast time on the Monday, and by dinner time on Friday he was the Champion Golfer. Into the narrow period of 108 hours, four

days and a half, he had crammed his first experience of
British courses—and that, many would insist, the most
difficult of all to master—his first experience of the British
ball, and his first experience of weather so severe that it
destroyed many great and famous players.

It is true that he had the best of the weather and the best
of caddies, but when every allowance is made, Lema
proved himself a golfer of rare quality. How did it come
about that this young man, of whom we had never heard
until two years ago, had acquired a method and a temperament that could withstand the rigours of our
weather, the challenge of the Old Course, and the tremendous pressure applied by the formidable Jack Nicklaus on that final day?

Lema freely admits that he has tried to learn from his
fellow-competitors on the tour. When he played practice
rounds with Byron Nelson and Ken Venturi before his
first Masters' Tournament last year, he asked Nelson for
his comments on his swing. The fact that Nelson told him
his swing could not be faulted from what he had seen of
it in three days' play did as much as anything to put Lema
second in his first Masters, just beaten by a putt by Nicklaus.

But the man from whom Lema, in common with many
other American professionals, learned most was Arnold
Palmer. What Palmer taught him was nothing to do with
hitting a golf ball. Lema used to be a wild character, hot-
tempered, volatile, given to rich and strange oaths when
shots went awry. Palmer once told him, in the friendliest
way, that there was no future in golf for anyone who
behaved as Lema did. Later, when Lema was slowly mas-
tering himself, it was Palmer who gave him what he calls
a "positive philosophy."

Near the end of one of his best seasons, Lema has written, Palmer summed up this philosophy: "I just kind of
see what it is I have to do, and I just make up my mind

that I'm going to do it. If I have a long putt to make I just think about making that putt. I shut from my mind the thought of missing it or all the other stuff that would come from my missing it." After that, said Lema, "I finished out the year in grand style."

Palmer, according to Lema, is "highly respected by every golfer on the tour because, in addition to being such a magnificent golfer, he is a very down-to-earth person. He was thoughtful and unselfish when he first came out on the tour, and his spectacular success has not changed him at all. Most of the touring pros agree that if fate had decreed one man must dominate the profession, then we are happy this role is played by Arnold."

Maybe, then, we in Britain are right in respecting and admiring Palmer so much; and if Lema comes back next year and plays as well and behaves as well as he did at St. Andrews, we shall bracket them together.

Possibly the last flash of the old Lema was displayed at the Masters last year. He was still very much in the running when he missed a short putt on the twelfth green in the final round.

"I barked out a stream of the filthiest language I had used since mustering out of the Marines in 1955," he writes. "When I straightened up I noticed my playing partner, a Formosan named Chen Ching-po, who was also having his troubles in the final round, looking at me in a funny way. I walked over to him and apologised for using such vile language in front of a visitor to my country.

"He smiled and then said in very broken English: 'Is all right. If I knew those words I would use them myself.'"

Match Play and Character (1965)

I hope no one will think the Americans have made a wise decision in announcing, as they did at the weekend, that this year their Amateur championship will be played by 72 holes of medal play* instead of by matches as has been the form since Charles Blair Macdonald beat Charles Sands at Newport by 12 and 11 exactly 70 years ago.

That was the first U.S. Amateur championship in the sense that it was run by the Amateur Golf Association of the United States, the forerunner of the U.S.G.A., but there had been two earlier tournaments run privately to determine the best amateur in the country and the first was, oddly, decided by medal play. So the Americans are now turning back the clock to the 1890s when Willie Lawrence, a local member, won at Newport with steady rounds of 93, 95 against Macdonald's 89, 100.

Perhaps if Macdonald had won that initial competition there would have been no tradition of match-play amateur championships in America. Charlie Macdonald had been educated at our St. Andrews, where he developed into a fine player, and he was, as he thought, cock of the golfing walk in America in the 1890s, though, to be sure, the walk was pretty circumscribed because there were so few courses and players.

He took it for granted that he would win an invitation tournament at Newport in September, 1894, the first competition of its kind ever held in the United States, and if he had, perhaps American amateurs would have decided their championships by strokes for ever after.

---

*The Amateur championship has since gone back to match play.

But Macdonald, though a good golfer, was a bad loser, and, when Lawrence beat him, he hollered loud and long that medal play was no proper method of determining an amateur champion—amateur championships in Britain were invariably match-play tournaments, and the Newport 36-hole medal competition should be ruled "no contest."

He stirred up so much controversy that the St. Andrew's Club of New York promptly promoted a match-play tournament within a matter of weeks in which 27 golfers set out to stop Macdonald. He began like a raging lion, won his first two matches easily, and then beat Lawrence in the semi-final. Alas, he lost at the nineteenth in the final to Laurence Stoddard, who had learned his golf at Hoylake, and then produced as good a crop of excuses as can be found in the whole calendar of sport.

He had been ill. He had been to a party given by the noted architect Stanford White (who was murdered by Harry Thaw in 1906), he had got to bed at five, he had taken strychnine pills to see him through his semi-final, and had taken White's advice to have a steak and champagne for lunch. It was this foolhardy lunch, he insisted, that made him slice his nineteenth-hole tee-shot into a ploughed field.

Any man who could trot out so many excuses deserved to win the first championship proper when it was played a year later, but he didn't deserve to win anymore than that—nor did he.

One man who would have supported Macdonald in his claims for match as against medal play was Freddie Tait, the best match-player of his time. Tait once wrote to a friend: "Why do you talk about the scoring game? There is no more game in scoring than in rifle-shooting." The fun for Tait was in beating his man, and this enjoyment was denied to the man who played for or against a score. As John L. Low put it, "The winner of a stroke competition only gets the verdict on points, he lacks the satisfaction of giving the knock-out blow."

For myself, I regard match play as being integral to amateur championships. Match play, it seems to me, demands certain qualities in a player that are indicative of his character. Golfers who are wonderful with card and pencil have been seen to blench when, playing in a match, their opponent has stuck a long approach up against the flag and they have to follow as best they may; or, more exquisite still, their ball is lying handy for the par figure or a birdie and the opponent comes from nowhere and stuffs in a long steal.

It is then that the true worth of a player is proclaimed. If he can match the unexpected blow, he is so much the better man, for the essential fact of golf as a game is when the player is subjected to pressures and emerges triumphant.

In any case, conflict is the essence of match play, and conflict as between man and man, not as between one man and the rest of the field spread over four rounds, is wonderfully well worth watching. I would cheerfully watch an Amateur championship in which I might hope to see some unknown fledgling strike down the soaring eagle; I would not walk the length of a putting green to see a group of scoring machines going through the motions day after day.

The winner in medal play might be the most complete executant, the most competent technician; he would not necessarily be the best golfer.

"To the Devil with Philosophy— I'm Trying to Play Golf" (1965)

Today I recall a man who derived more aesthetic and spiritual delight from conflict on the links than anyone else I have played with: Hector Hetherington.

The late Principal of Glasgow University was devoted to golf. He was never happier than when playing, and although in a very full life he had little time for the larger leisure of the links, he never let slip the smallest opportunity of exercising his wholly remarkable skill.

As a young man he was a very accomplished player and, in rare moments of confession, he would admit to having had a handicap of 2. According to one biographical notice in a journal that should know the facts of his life, he had competed in the Amateur championship; but he was never given to proclaiming his virtues, and his closest golfing companion of the last 30 years has no personal proof of Hector's having enjoyed that status.

I played with him only rarely, occasionally on a Sunday afternoon at Killermont when he would play just as many holes as he had time for. The weather did not matter. If the course was playable, and there was an hour or so to spare, Hector would don what Lionel Munn used to call his "doivin' suit" and set out, a small bag under his arm, supremely happy, and, even when he was in his seventies, supremely capable.

It mattered little to Hector that he had lost his length with the years. He would cheerfully tackle the longish uphill sixth hole with three wooden club shots and then, having arrived at the middle of the green, he was as likely as not to hole the putt. He dearly loved being teased about approaching the green with his brassie.

Once I played a full round with him and other companions at Gailes. It was a difficult day and Hector was not at his best off the tee, which made Gailes an affair of energy and frustration. At one hole where he was plowtering about in the heather and saluting his efforts at recovery with most unacademic language, I suggested, greatly daring, that for a man of his scholastic background he was adopting a most unphilosophic attitude. His reply was in character: "To the devil with philosophy. I'm trying to play golf!"

Of all games that he played in a long life, those he enjoyed most were for the Senate of Glasgow University against their Aberdeen counterparts. This is a match of the most respectable antiquity. It was started in the 1880s and is played annually, one year in Aberdeen, the other in or near Glasgow.

Those with the necessary qualifications wear a spectacular tie, but the tie is not lightly granted. There is no question of a man's playing once, as he does for his country, and thus earning the right to wear the tie forever and a day. They observe a sterner rigour at Glasgow and Aberdeen. You have to play twice in an away match before the tie is yours, which means that even the best of players could be four years at their university before they win the qualification if in their first year the contest is played on their home turf.

When he returned to Glasgow in 1924 to the Chair of Moral Philosophy, he was an immediate choice for the match at Aberdeen. At that time the individual games were decided by the number of holes up, which gave point to the old exhortation: "Make every hole a winning hole." The Professor of Midwifery at Aberdeen had some responsibility for the placing of his side and selected as his own opponent the young Professor of Philosophy, of whom he had never heard. Hector won the match by 14 up and was, of course, a marked man thereafter.

He liked to play golf; he liked almost as much to talk about it and to hear it discussed. It was for that reason that he and other members of the Senate who shared his enthusiasms made a splendid gesture some years ago to three members of the General Council—that is to say, graduates—who had in their time been chosen to play for Britain in the Walker Cup match. The three were Dr. Frank Deighton, R. Reid Jack, and your correspondent.

We were entertained to dinner in the College Club, and Hector, in the chair, made one of his urbane, delightful speeches that had all the air of being impromptu but that had entailed more preparation than one would have thought a busy man would have the time and inclination for.

Then we had a wonderful round-table discussion over which Hector presided, beaming, and which did not end until Dr. Deighton had taken his dinner-jacket off and was demonstrating the mechanics of the swing to an audience of physicists, pathologists, Shakespearean scholars, engineers, and theologians.

It could have been said of Hector what had been said about another well-known professor's golf: "He knew and loved this game and played it with skill, judgment, and a touch of bravado under pressure."

The World Champion Hider of Drinks (1966)

In the 1930s Fred Corcoran, golf's most successful impresario, became tournament manager for the American professionals as a body, promoted the circuit of big-money events, managed American Ryder Cup teams, knew everybody and was known by everybody from presidents of chambers of commerce down to the rawest caddie.

He is full of good stories and shrewd observations, and one of his tales that I liked better than most concerned an old friend, opponent, and hero of my own—Walter Hagen, better known as "The Haig." Hagen was also not a bad player, and he was the begetter of some memorable phrases, not least this comment on his ambitions: "I don't want to be a millionaire, I just want to live like one."

Corcoran, in a book called "Unplayable Lies", demolishes one of the legends that grew up around Hagen when he was possibly the best known golfer in the world and certainly the game's most picturesque personality. Hagen was reputed to be a good-time golfer, the Champagne Tony of his time, only his taste in refreshment was the wine of our country, not France.

But, insists Corcoran, "The legend has distorted the actual portrait. True, Hagen loved life and people. And he hated to go to bed because sleeping seemed like such a waste of time. But the picture of Hagen flashing through life with champagne bubbling out of his ears is a false one. The Hagen of his golden years took excellent care of himself."

"He was the world's champion hider of drinks. Walter always had a full glass in his hand. But after the ball was over, the sweeper would find a dozen drinks lined up behind the piano where Hagen had slyly stashed them during the revels." (Corcoran does not say where Hagen put the drinks in a room where there was no piano, but we can let that pass.)

This picture of Hagen agreed with my own view of him. When the American Ryder Cup team met a West of Scotland amateur side at Whitecraigs in 1933, I was drawn against the great man. At lunch he sent me a pencilled note, I being well below the salt, suggesting that we play for a shilling a hole.

At present-day prices, that would be about 5s a hole, but the price seemed to me a small one at the time, and I was heartened by the sight of Hagen in the place of honour with, every time I looked towards him, a full libation at his right hand. But there must have been a piano in the Whitecraigs dining-room, for Hagen began with two birdies.

In the 1929 British Open, Leo Diegel, it may be remembered, led the field after 36 holes with 71, 69, with Hagen two shots behind and our own Abe Mitchell third, two behind Hagen. Around one o'clock in the morning Hagen was holding court (and a glass in his hand)in the hotel lounge when some one suggested that it was time he was in bed—with 36 holes to be played that day and the wind already rising.

"Besides," came the clincher, "Diegel's been in bed for a couple of hours." "Sure," said Walter, "Diegel's in bed—but he's not sleeping." And, then, I have no doubt, he put another glass behind the piano.

An Unobtrusive Golfer (1966)

During the war, I watched a charity cricket match at Warrington between teams captained by George Duckworth, who died the other day, and Learie Constantine.

Constantine, the West Indian, was one of the greatest cricketers of all time. That day, he scored next to nothing, took no wickets, and his fielding, though effortlessly competent, produced no spectacular catch or thrilling run-out.

Yet when he was on the field, it was impossible to see anyone else. He did not play to the gallery, there were no extravagances of gesture, not even a flashing smile when things went right—or wrong. But somehow his tremendous personality communicated itself to everyone on and around the pitch.

Some golfers are like Constantine, Arnold Palmer, for example. When they are in action, they have to be seen and savoured.

There is another type of golfer, possibly just as efficient, with just as good a record of achievement, but lacking that spark which sets the crowd alight. One such Scottish golfer died last week, as unobtrusively as he lived and played. He was Robert Scott, who for most of his long life was known as R. Scott, Jr. because his father, himself a golfer of persistence and some skill, lived to a great age.

Bob Scott's chief claim to fame, though he was never heard himself to make the claim, was that he was the other Glasgow golfer who beat Bobby Jones.

The whole world knows that Andrew Jamieson beat Jones in the Amateur championship at Muirfield in 1926, when Jamieson was only a stripling and Jones, though only 24, had already won two American Amateur championships and one U.S. Open title.

It was one of the most spectacular successes ever achieved by a young Scottish golfer and was none the less meritorious because Jones had a stiff neck that day and his glorious swing lacked something of its fluidity and grace.

Bob Scott's triumph over the great American was not, like Jamieson's, in single-handed combat, but in the final analysis the issue depended on the play of the two men rather than of their partners.

The occasion was the third Walker Cup match at Garden City, in which Bob Scott and his namesake, the Honourable Michael Scott, met in the third foursome Jones and W. C. Fownes, who had captained the U.S. side in the inaugural match two years earlier.

At one stage the British pair were three down, but they fought back so resolutely that they were square with only the last hole, a short one, to play. Bob Scott and Jones had to play the tee-shot, and it was Scott who produced a beauty which Jones could not match. So, in a sense, he beat Bobby Jones just as surely as did Jamieson two years later, for it must have been a forbidding experience, with all to play for, having to go first against the young master who the year before had won the American Open championship.

That, incidentally, was the only time Jones was beaten in five Walker Cup matches, and as the American also won both his games in the 1921 International before the Walker Cup series was started, Scott's distinction was very real.

Bob Scott had earned his place in the 1924 British team by virtue of two excellent achievements in 1922 and 1923. In 1922 he reached the semi-final of the Amateur championship at Prestwick, beating on the way the favourite, Roger Wethered, who had so nearly won the Open championship the year before.

John Caven beat Scott by one hole in a fine semi-final match fought, as "The Glasgow Herald" reporter put it on the morrow of the game, "in the friendliest possible spirit. . . . When Caven holed a short putt to reach the finals of the Amateur for the first time in his life, Scott threw down his putter and shook Caven warmly with both hands. Then arm in arm they walked into the clubhouse, and, if you did not know, you could not have told which one was the loser."

Who would not rather have had that said of him than been praised for winning?

Scott showed a year later that his play at Prestwick had been no isolated week of brilliance. In the Open championship at Troon Scott finished first amateur.

So he was quite a player, and he kept his swing and his game for a very long time. I used to see him often at Killermont (he joined the Glasgow Club in 1902), a sturdy stocky figure with an easy, compact swing that invariably despatched the ball right down the track. He played with no fuss at all. He made the game look the easiest possible exercise, and with his small bag tucked under his arm had all the appearance of a countryman walking the fields with his gun.

When he was in his sixties he brought in a very low score in a medal. This was reported to his father in the clubhouse, and evoked the wonderful comment, "Why shouldn't he? He's got youth on his side."

The Best Lesson I Ever Had (1969)

Last summer I was one of a group of people instrumental in doing an act of kindness to an elderly golfer.

It was a heavenly day on Speyside and we, wives and all, were bound for Boat of Garten Golf Club to let me have my first game on that delectable course, which is a sort of scaled-down Rosemount. On our way we encountered a motorist stranded with a puncture, and common charity, plus the fact that he was elderly and wore a clerical collar and a bewildered look, obliged us to stop and offer aid.

Happily in our company were two men skilled in such matters, and although the tools were rusty and the housing of the jack flimsier than any manufacturer had the right to produce, all in the end was well, the tire was changed, and he was ready for the road again.

I had noticed that his only luggage was a meagre golf bag in the boot, and he vouchsafed the information that he was going to Newtonmore to play golf. He was so grateful for our help that, as Wordsworth would have put it, my 'winsome marrow' said we, too, were bound for golf, at "the Boat," and she suggested that he might "put in a word for their putting."

"Ah," he said with a grave twinkle, "I am reluctant to involve the Almighty in golf."

It reminded me irresistibly, if irreverently, of an episode in the career of Gary Player, who suffers from no such inhibitions as the Roman Catholic canon we succoured in Speyside. When Player won the Masters tournament at Augusta, in 1961, he went so far as to say at the presentation that "from the moment I came to Augusta this year I felt that the Lord wanted me to win."

A cynical member of Arnie's army was heard to remark in the loudest of stage whispers that the Lord must have wanted Arnie to lose, for Palmer, it may be remembered, "had only" to do the last hole in 4 to win, bunkered his second, and then contrived to pitch over the green, take two more to hole out, and thus make a virtual gift of the tournament to Player.

The little South African was unabashed. He was persuaded in his own mind that the Lord wanted him to win, and win he did, as the records show. But his declaration of faith was not forgotten.

When he arrived the following year at Augusta he was asked by a newspaperman with a long memory and a sceptical mind, "Well, Gary, does the Lord want you to win this year?" And Player replied, in all seriousness, "I don't think quite so much this time."

He was right, too. He didn't win, but he came precious close to it, finishing in a tie with Palmer and Finsterwald for first place, a tie that Palmer won on the playoff.

When I was only a boy, rejoicing in all a boy's enthusiasms and wallowing in his despairs, I played in a stroke competition at Millport with an elderly little man whom I had seen puttering about in the bay in a canoe-shaped boat equipped with a temperamental outboard motor that he seemed ill-equipped to control.

His golf was no better than his mastery of mechanics, and I was disposed to blame my own sloppy play on his own indifferent performance. When I took an abysmal three putts on the ninth green I exploded, and involved the Almighty and all the hosts of Heaven and Hell in my sorry game.

Then HE exploded. He rent me in twain; denounced me for taking the Lord's name in vain, told me to pull myself together and stop playing rubbish, my score was not all that bad, and if I played as he knew I could play, I could even now win the competition.

It was a very chastened boy who drove off the tenth tee but, wonder of wonders, my game came back to me, I holed a few putts, and no one was more pleased than my fellow-competitor when I knocked in a long one on the last green and won the sweepstake.

Since then I have never walked along Ingram Street in Glasgow without remembering that lesson, the best I ever had, from the Rev. John A. Swan, who was at the time minister of that venerable foundation on the north side of the thoroughfare.

Many times since then I have been just as angry with myself as I was that day at Millport, and no doubt I have been just as guilty as the next golfer of blaming my imperfections on something other than my own frailty. But Mr. Swan caught me in time, I like to think, and the right time at that.

He Made the Game Look Hard (1969)

There is rare irony in the fact that the World Match-Play championship was won last week by a stone-faced quiet man only a few days after the death of the greatest professional match-player of them all, who was anything but a quiet man.

No doubt, if Bob Charles had played the same brand of golf against Hagen which destroyed his rivals at Wentworth, Hagen, too, would have succumbed. After all, he had been thrashed in his day, even in his heyday. Compston massacred him in a famous match at Moor Park. George Duncan mauled him 10 and 8 in the Ryder Cup at Moortown.

But Hagen, as all the world remembers, went straight from Moor Park to Sandwich and won the Open by two strokes from Sarazen, three from Compston. And he went from Moortown to Muirfield and won his fourth, and possibly best, Open by the length of a street.

Oddly, the men who beat Hagen were very far from being quiet men. Compston was big, raw-boned, immensely strong, and as extrovert as Hagen. Duncan, the professionals' professional, was tabbed throughout his career as "mercurial." At his best he was unbeatable, at his worst unbelievable. He was at his best against Hagen.

It should be remembered, too, that when Hagen lost to Compston by 18 and 17, there were no big jets to sweep the invaders across the Atlantic in not much more time than it takes an American four-ball game to circumnavigate the course. Hagen was just off the boat, in a manner of speaking, and before he caught the boat he had been cavorting before the cameras in Hollywood. He was therefore ill-prepared for his joust with Compston, though the big Englishman was at his best and that was terribly good.

Why, then, did Hagen so capture the imagination of the golfing world, in the same way as Palmer, of our generation, has become a folk-hero of the links? Why would I rather have watched either struggle to a 78 instead of watching the cool technicians such as Charles and Littler travel as though in predestinate perfection to a 66?

It is not just because Charles never "bares a fang," as one American matron put it. Henry Cotton was no laughing boy when he was standing astride the British golf scene like a Colossus. He looked more like Buster Keaton than any man had a right to look. Yet Cotton was rich in personality and always at the heart of controversy.

James Braid, to go back still farther, was a solemn, stately figure, who never played to the gallery. It was once said of him that no one could be so wise as James Braid looked, yet he was held in high esteem and affection by people who had never touched the hem of his garment.

It was a wise American who put his over-40 finger on what made Hagen so outstanding a personality. He was interesting to watch because he made the game look hard. The other star golfers made the game look easy: all you had to do was knock the ball down the fairway, pitch it on the green, and get down in two putts. But Hagen? Once or twice a round he hooked or sliced a drive as savagely as a 90-golfer, leaving himself a shot that looked absolutely unplayable until he executed a fantastic recovery.

These violent errors by a champion had the same effect on the spectators as if they had watched a supposedly flawless tightrope-walker suddenly lose his balance and go hurtling through space into the net below. Then when the performer went back to his perch and this time successfully waltzed on the wire, the spectators realised how hard it really was to walk a tightrope, or play par golf.

You almost get the same sensation watching Palmer. He

hits thrilling shots, and they are always hit hard. He hits the odd outrageous shot, and then he is at his most dangerous. He wears his heart on his sleeve, success or failure is written on his broad, homely face, and you identify with him in a way which I defy anyone to identify with the impassive perfectionists such as Charles and Littler.

They are beautiful golfers. The shots are superb, the errors rare. And they putt like Locke. But they are inhumanly good. They are not even accomplished gamesmen, partly because they are so efficient that they need no adventitious aids to success.

Hagen was a great gamesman. He could outthink his opponents if he could not outplay them. He reminded me, however unlikely the parallel may seem, of the great W. G. Grace, the monumental bearded giant of English cricket at the end of the century.

Grace, I read somewhere, had scored a century on every county ground but one, and this time he got to 98. So he asked the opposing captain if he would get the bowler to send up a full toss so that he could get his hundred—"and then I'll get out." Up came the full toss, Grace cracked it for 4, of course "didn't get out," and went on to score 189.

Hagen would have loved that. He thought nothing of whipping out an iron for his second shot when his ball was only a few feet past his opponent's. His opponent, who knew in his heart he needed a brassie, was shamed into taking an iron, and finishing hopelessly short. Back went Hagen's iron, out came his brassie, and he fired it into the heart of the green. Then he grinned all over his sunburned face.

He would certainly have subscribed to the dictum—"Never give a sucker an even break." I think, too, he would have taken the quiet men of golf by the seat of their tailored pants and beaten some life into them if he couldn't beat the golfing life out of them.

Links Lawyers (1969)

Willie Auchterlonie should be living at this hour. I would dearly like to have heard his comments on last week's announcement from the Royal and Ancient that prize money in next year's Open championship on the St. Andrews Old Course he knew and loved so well will amount to £40,000.

I choose Willie Auchterlonie of the old-time winners not because he was the last home-based Scot to win the championship—in 1893—but because from his own lips I heard what he had won by his victory at Prestwick with a total of 322 for four rounds that would not rate as a respectable score by a moderate amateur to-day.

Willie's first prize was £30, handsome enough by the standards of those days, no doubt, but meagre to our way of thinking. Even if we make every allowance for the change in the value of money, the most generous estimate of what £30 in 1893 might be worth today could hardly put it as high as £300—and that's what the man who finishes 22nd next year will get.

Don't, I beg you, think that I deplore this development. The labourer is worthy of his hire, etc., and the professional of great skill and courage is entitled to be rewarded for his excellence.

It was manifestly absurd even in Walter Hagen's day that first prize in the greatest championship in the world should be so small that the winner could afford to give the cheque to his caddie for his fee. True, only a showman such as Hagen would think of making the gesture, but the fact that he made it was a measure of the rewards then available to the masters of the links.

But this vast increase in prize money has brought with

it one development that is not wholly desirable. The professional who makes a mistake—in play or in interpreting the rules—can be heavily penalized financially. In the result the professionals have become links lawyers who not only know the rules but are alert to every advantage that a strict interpretation may allow them.

We have travelled a very long way from the days when the up-and-coming James Braid was playing a money match with the redoubtable and established J. H. Taylor.

Towards the end of the match, when any mistake might have been fatal, Braid, in addressing his ball, touched it. He was a pillar of integrity, and he immediately called over to Taylor that he had touched his ball but was not sure whether he had moved it.

"Never mind, Jimmy," said Taylor, "just play on."

A Lesson in Manners—from an American (1970)

The other day I was playing in a four-ball match of little consequence but large enjoyment when I found myself at a critical stage faced with a pitch of some delicacy.

There was precious little room to come and go on if the ball was to get near enough the hole to make putting on winter greens relatively secure. I knew what to do, but could not at the last screw my courage to the sticking point.

As a result, I played a shot that was neither one thing nor another and the ball finished a long way from the hole. My dissatisfaction was in no way diminished when I heard an almost stentorian comment, "Miles short."

It did not come, as well it might, from my long-suffering partner or even, gleefully, from either of our opponents. It came from someone on a tee nearby, and, bless my soul, I had never seen the commentator in my life. The episode rankled and I indicated as much to an understanding friend some days later. "Ah," he said, "but you wouldn't have minded a bit if you had played a good shot and your unknown commentator had saluted the stroke with 'Good shot.'"

He was, of course, right, for I would have purred with satisfaction that a stranger had been impressed by my expertise, but I still cling to the truth of the old tag that "There's a time to speak and a time to be silent."

Comment on the course, whether from a companion or from the crowd, is sometimes ill to deal with. For example, not until I played with a Southern gentleman in the United States did I know what to say to a partner or fellow-competitor if he chose to compliment me on a stroke.

Usually I muttered something like "Oh, it's not bad," even if the shot was of superlative excellence.

We Scots are not very gracious in receiving compliments. The North Carolina golfer had a much simpler formula. The first time I played with him he came up with a beautiful long iron to the second green, the sort of shot I would have given my weak left hand for, and I was moved to exclaim, "Good shot." He replied, "Thank you," and really what more could any man say? In accepting my compliment he paid me a compliment.

Sometimes an opponent's comment can be a powerful stimulus. Once I was playing in a match at Hoylake with the redoubtable Jock Smith of Elie as my partner. We were one up after 11 holes on two young English sprigs, one of whom was asked by a friend as we approached the twelfth green how the match stood.

"Oh," he said with what Smith and I thought to be altogether too casual a nonchalance, "we're one down—just now," as much as to say "We've got the beating of these two. It's only a matter of time." So Smith pulled down his brows, grunted even louder as he thumped his next drive, and, when it finished only a yard or so behind the booming tee-shot of his young opponent, confided in me in a loud enough voice to be heard across the Sands of Dee, "He's no giein' the auld fella much, is he?"

Vardon and Jones (1970)

Bobby Jones is 68 today, St. Patrick's Day, and all golfers of good will should be united in wishing him well. He was in his day the greatest of players, and in his long retirement from active golf he has won almost as much respect and affection as when he bestrode the links like a Colossus.

I remember his birthday because of a moment during the Walker Cup match at Sandwich in 1930, when he captained the American team. On his key chain there hung what I took to be a gold four-leafed clover, and it seemed odd to me that this great player should be, like the rest of us, influenced by charms and good-luck tokens.

A more knowledgeable friend pointed out, however, that the adornment was a shamrock, not a clover, and that Bobby wore it by right of birth. Maybe it brought him the luck of the Irish in his playing days, but it has brought him singularly little luck these last 20 years and more.

This year he is almost certain to miss for the second time the Masters Tournament at Augusta which more than anyone else he helped to create and build into something very close to a world championship.

Bobby—or Bob as he is known in his own country—will be the last to grieve.

He was, of course, the supreme competitor. Every schoolboy knows his record, or, if he does not, he should be ordered to study the record books and wonder that any one man could win in the space of only eight years, from 1923 to 1930, no fewer than 13 major championships, and one of these, the British Amateur championship, he won only once.

So he was only 28 when he retired, full of honours, and at the very peak of his fame, for in that final year 1930, his *annus mirabilis*, he won the Open and Amateur championships of both Britain and the United States in one short summer.

Jones had so many claims to distinction as a golfer that it came as only a mild realization to me the other day that he was in fact a link between two important eras of the game. He stamped his own name and his supreme elegance and excellence on the third decade of the century, but he was also a bridge between the great days of the Triumvirate and the equally great days (as I insist they were) of the modern masters, Hogan, Nelson, and Cotton.

Jones touched the fringe of the Palmer-Nicklaus era only by his presence at the Masters when they were the heroic figures, but he played in the 1938 Masters, the first year that Hogan played, and it was the old master who played right through the tournament and the new and little-known Hogan who failed to make the "cut."

Jones also played with Vardon, whose centenary falls in May, and thereby hangs a tale that reveals a good deal about both men. In the qualifying round for the U.S. Open at Inverness in 1920, the 18-year-old wonder from Atlanta was paired with the visiting lion, then a ripe but still formidable 50.

On the seventh hole, a drive-and-pitch par 4, Vardon made his par with all the ease that was his hallmark. Jones, at times a little vulnerable on mashie-niblick pitches, looked up on the shot, hit it thin over the green, and took 5. As they walked to the next tee, Jones, trying to dispel his embarrassment, said to Vardon, "Have you ever seen a worse shot than that, sir?" "No," answered Vardon, and nothing more.

He might, I think, have been a little more generous if only for the "sir," but at least he was nothing like so shattering as he was in replying to another American with whom he played on an earlier tour of America, in 1913, the year when Francis Ouimet beat both Vardon and Ted Ray in a play-off for the U.S. Open championship at Brookline and, in the process, played shots which rang round the world.

It was at Chicago, in that 1913 tour, that Vardon found himself in a four-ball game with a left-hander of no especial merit who, however, had his day of days and played so far above himself that he was rash enough to address the master: "If I may be so bold, Mr. Vardon, might I inquire who is the best left-handed golfer you've come across in your long career?" Vardon snorted. "Never saw one who was worth a damn," he said.

I wonder if those who watched Vardon and Jones together at Inverness realised that they were seeing one who had been the greatest playing with one who was to become possibly even greater. Luckily for me I had a glimpse of Vardon in 1919 in a tournament at Killermont, and even as a small boy I was aware of the grace and elegance which caused him to be dubbed the Jersey Greyhound (he was born at Grouville, in the Channel Island of Jersey). And I saw Jones at his peak. No one would be so rash as to compare Vardon with Jones. They were the best in their day, champions for all time.

Palmer (1971)

For one who has done so much and won so much over such a long period, Palmer has retained to a wonderful degree an acceptable public image. After all, he won his first major tournament, the United States Amateur championship, as long ago as 1954. He won his first Masters tournament in 1958, his first (and only) U.S. Open championship in 1960, his first (of two) British Opens in 1961.

That is a very long time to be at the heart of such a public affair as tournament golf, and it is perhaps rather surprising that only now has he been awarded the Bob Jones award for "distinguished sportsmanship." The award will be presented in New York at the 77th annual meeting of the United States Golf Association on the last Saturday of this month, and the great man will, of course, be there for the great occasion.

This is a very special kind of award. It was conceived to commemorate the great contributions to the cause of fair play on and off the links made by Robert Tyre Jones, Jr., the nonpareil of golf. It postulates in the winner personal qualities that are esteemed in sport, any sport anywhere.

The U.S.G.A. lists these qualities as "fair play, self-control, perhaps self-denial, generosity of spirit towards an opponent or towards the game as a whole, manner of playing or behaving so as to show respect for the game and the people in it, and unselfishness."

No one would claim, least of all Palmer himself, that throughout his long career he has always and uniformly displayed those qualities. He has had his lapses, especially of self-control, as what red-blooded golfer has not. He would have had to be an angel not to show dismay, even temper, when a bad stroke ruined a round or a seemingly good stroke was harshly treated by the terrain.

That happened to Palmer at Troon in the 1962 Open when the course was iron-hard after a drought and the kittle kinks of the fairways sent the best shots into the worst places. He tells in "My Game and Yours" of just such an incident.

"One day, on the fifteenth, I hit what I think was probably the finest drive of my life, long and absolutely square, right down the centre of the fairway on the exact line I had planned as the maximum protection against trouble. Yet when I got to the ball I found that it had bounced all the way off the fairway and into a thick tangle of downhill rough—as nasty a lie as anyone ever suffered for a roundhouse slice or a horrible hook."

No one is going to tell me that Arnold smiled happily when he found his ball. There must have been at the least a monumental frown—and, goodness, his frown is intimidating. But he had the self-control to make the best of a bad situation, and all his wonderful life of achievement he has been doing just that.

Listen to what his great friend and rival, Jack Nicklaus, has written about the man who dominated a decade on the golf courses of the world: "He is an unusually appealing fellow; a handsome, clean-cut athlete, confident in his abilities but modest about them, natural in manner, very well-spoken, and, with all this, endowed with a rare brand of magnetism.

"He created the perfect image for the modern professional golfer . . . He also evoked the ideal atmosphere for modern professional golf: it was a game for gentlemen, played in beautiful surroundings, but a wearing, demanding game that might erupt at any moment into high drama. I don't think there is any question whatsoever that all of us who have flourished in golf in recent years owe Arnold Palmer a great deal."

Now that is handsomely spoken and no more than the truth from an essentially truthful person. Palmer is one of the milestones in golf. Just as Vardon, Braid, and Taylor made professional golf respectable in Britain, and Hagen and Cotton showed that professionals deserved not only approbation but a place in society on and off the course, so Palmer has elevated the American professional to a standing in the whole world which no other class or kind of sportsmen can hope to occupy.

Palmer in action is one of the great sporting sights of our times. It is not just that he plays fantastic shots, that he has holed more important putts than probably anyone of his generation, that he has won everything there is to win except his own P.G.A. championship.

He carries about with him an aura of excitement, this magnificently built athlete with the purposeful stride, the friendly grin when things are going well, the rueful grin when things go awry. Even the way he hitches up his pants communicates something to the crowd, and he has just to play one daring, successful stroke for the crowd to roar its appreciation.

I remember seeing him play in the Masters and having a struggling round until he holed a beast of a cross-hill putt for a birdie at the seventh. He thrust himself on to the tee of the long, uphill eighth, unleashed a tremendous drive, and, immediately after his fellow-competitor had driven, Palmer was off like—as I wrote at the time— Teddy Roosevelt charging up San Juan hill.

It was immensely thrilling, but it will be a thrill of a different, more enduring kind when Palmer steps up to receive the Bob Jones award. No one deserves it more.

You Can't Choose the Best (1971)

In "Thirty Years of Championship Golf," arguably the best single volume on golf ever written, Gene Sarazen includes a chapter on the masters of modern golf in which he classifies the great players of his time.

He put Jones and Hagen in the highest class, modestly excluding himself, and among six in the second class he included Hogan, Henry Cotton, and Sam Snead. He was writing, of course, in 1950, before Hogan had won three more American Open championships and, best of all, his British Open championship at Carnoustie.

Those achievements would undoubtedly put Hogan into the same bracket as Jones and Hagen, because Sarazen's criterion of preeminence was the number of major championships won. If he were rewriting the book today he would upgrade Palmer, who in 1950 had won only the U.S. Amateur championship, and he would inevitably include Nicklaus on the top rung of the ladder.

He might even build an extension and put Nicklaus at the very top, though he would never go so far as did the commentator on the American P.G.A. championship won last week in Florida by Nicklaus, and describe him as the greatest golfer there has ever been.

The greatest golfer playing today, perhaps, nay almost certainly, but the greatest there has ever been? Sarazen twenty years ago gave the only sensible answer: "I honestly do not know who would have beaten whom—the Hagen of 1924, the Jones of 1930, the Nelson of 1945, or the Hogan of 1948. It would have depended, probably, on what day it was." And possibly on the kind of competition, the kind of course, the kind of weather.

All that one can say of the greatest player of his time is

what was said of Tom Cribb, the pugilist, after he had beaten Molineaux for the second time. It was decided that he need never fight again but should bear the title of Champion to the end of his days.

We can say that of Hagen, of Jones, of Sarazen himself (who, after all, won all the major American titles and also our "Open"), of Palmer, and now of Nicklaus. In Britain we can say it of the Triumvirate and of Henry Cotton who were in their day the nonpareils, and it could be said, too, of Michael Bonallack in amateur golf.

But it is no more possible to compare Nicklaus at his best with even Hogan at his best than it is to compare either with Jones or Hagen. Personally I would have backed Hagen at his best to beat Hogan and even Nicklaus, setting aside the inevitable improbabilities of such matches, but I am not sure that Hagen would have beaten Palmer.

It is an agreeable if profitless speculation to measure the modern masters against those of an earlier generation, and all that one can say with truth is that we are fortunate in having seen so many brilliant golfers in the last half-century.

Here, I realise, I speak only for a minority who are old enough to have seen and relished the great players whose achievements are the backbone of the record books. I was exceptionally fortunate in that as a little boy in short trousers with a vast capacity for hero-worship I saw Vardon, Taylor, and Braid playing at Killermont in a Victory tournament in 1919. On the same day I saw Duncan and Mitchell, and if that was too much fine feeding for the young mind, it was at least a point of departure for later studies of the great Americans who made their annual sorties in our championships.

It is against this background that I can appraise the achievements of Jack Nicklaus, who has now won 11 major championships and who must have every chance of surpassing Jones's record of 13. Time is on his side, but I must make the point that Jones accomplished his incomparable record in only eight years whereas Nicklaus won his first championship in 1959.

I can well remember seeing a photograph in the spring of 1923 of "Two great golfers who have never won a championship"—Roger Wethered and Bobby Jones. And that year Wethered won our "Amateur" at Deal and Jones won the first of his four American "Opens" at Inwood.

Once Jones began winning he kept on winning, and when he retired from amateur golf full of honours in 1930 he was only 28. Nicklaus is two years older, but, then, he started his championship career later than Jones—one year later.

Jones was only 14 when he played in his first U.S. Amateur championship, and he was even then so good that he was a possible winner. But in the third round he came up against Robert Gardner (who was later to lose to Tolley in the "Amateur" final at Muirfield in 1920), and lost a game he should have won.

Nicklaus was 15 when he played in his first U.S. Amateur championship and he lost by one hole in the first round—to Robert Gardner, same name, different generation.

The Finest Man I Ever Met (1971)

To me it is a little sad that a whole generation of players have grown up who never saw Bobby Jones play, who have to be content with reading of his exploits, of his marvellous record of championship victories. The last time he played in this country was 35 years ago, when he was on his way to the Olympic Games at Berlin and, while staying at Gleneagles Hotel for a few days, went to St. Andrews and played with Willie Auchterlonie and the late Gordon Lockhart.

I had heard that he was at Gleneagles, telephoned him to say "Hello," learned that he was going to St. Andrews on the morrow, and mentioned the fact in this paper. As a result 2000 people turned up to watch him.

It was a little unkind to make so public what he had hoped would be a private affair, but such was the magic of his name that the crowds thronged to see him. And he played like the old master he was, going out in 32 and, on the way, playing to the short eighth hole a shot of such superlative quality that his caddie was moved to murmur, "My, but you're a wonder, sir."

He took 40 to come home, largely because he took a 5 at the short eleventh where, as a very young and erratic man in 1921, he had picked up his ball in the Open championship. But that was before he came to know and love the Old Course, and I like to think that the course and the crowd were kind to him on his last playing visit.

The crowds were so hero-worshipping, in fact, in 1936 that he had to sign autographs for an interminable period after his game and had to be rescued by R. and A. officials. He was that kind of man—invariably kind and courteous. As Sarazen put it, "Bob was a fine man to be partnered with in a tournament. Congenial and considerate, he made you feel that you were playing with a friend, and you were."

He was uniformly kind to me. In the spring of last year I wrote a piece on his 68th birthday (St. Patrick's Day) suggesting that all golfers of good will should be united in wishing him well and recalling some of the great moments of his career. A fortnight later I had a generous letter from him, he having seen the article sent to him by an unknown friend in Lanarkshire—unknown to Bobby, unknown to me.

The last time I saw him was at the Masters tournament in 1966 when we were seated near each other at the dinner given to amateur players and some others on the eve of the tournament. He was then, after many years of illness, a wreck of a man physically, unable even to light his cigarette; but the mind was as clear as it ever was—and Sarazen said that "he had the finest mind of any competitive golfer."

His concern for the greatness of the game was still intense, he asked after his friends at St. Andrews and elsewhere in Scotland, and was in particular concerned to know whether I had appreciated how he had built into the Augusta course some of the essential character of the St. Andrews links which he loved this side of idolatry.

There he was, chairman at a dinner full of talent and famous names, and his thoughts were on the greater good of the great game. It sent my mind back to the first time I had met him, at the very place where he developed the game that sent the name of Bobby Jones ringing round the world.

In 1946 I visited the United States for the first time and went to Atlanta for a few days, primarily to see Charlie Yates. The first thing Charlie said when we met was, "Let's go out to East Lake and see Bob." We did, and when we arrived Jones had just finished a round with

Watts Gunn, who had played in the Walker Cup matches in 1926 and 1928 and, indeed, in the 1926 match had partnered Jones in the foursomes against Cyril Tolley and Andrew Jamieson.

So there we were, four Walker Cup players in the same locker-room, and you can imagine what the talk was about. But Jones's immediate concern was when we could play together—yes, he and I—and it will be my enduring regret that he could not play until the following Tuesday, by which time I had to be back in New York to catch the Queen Elizabeth's sailing.

I saw him again a few years later at the Peachtree Club, by which time he had undergone the surgery which left him a cripple for the last 20 years of his life, and I can recall as though it were yesterday how he took from his own neck the club tie and gave it to me as a memento of Peachtree. To me it was a memento of the greatest golfer I ever saw—and the finest man I ever met.

Absent Thee from Felicity Awhile (1972)

An East Coast golfer of some local renown gave up golf for no particular or convincing reason. He lost his taste for the game, and for seven long years literally did not touch a club. At Christmas he came through to the West of Scotland for a family reunion and a good time was had by all—such a good time, in fact, that he took little persuasion to make up a four at his host's course on the morning after.

There he soon learned that, as the road-safety exhortations remind us, you can't drink and drive. In short, he played so badly that his host's insistence to their companions that the errant one was really—or rather had been—a very good player fell on deaf ears.

Stung by failure, or perhaps bitten again by the bug, the quondam golfer sallied forth again two days later with his host and the two same companions, and this time he put away all childish things and went round in as near par as made no difference.

I believe the story implicitly, and not just because I am a sucker for romantic tales. It chimes with my own experience and the experience of many acquaintances, though comparatively few dedicated golfers have had to abjure the delights and miseries of the game for as long as seven years.

I remember immediately after the Second World War playing at Killermont with a man having his first game after having served six years in the Forces. Part of the time he had been a POW, and not in Stalag Luft III where some zealots, including the distinguished writer Pat Ward-Thomas, played golf in the compound with clubs and balls of their own making.

My friend had literally not struck a ball for six years and it was wholly fascinating to see him take the tee aquiver with eagerness. He had a few tentative practice swings and then hit a beauty down the middle, and he didn't know whether to laugh or cry. He played well enough to feel that the long years had not been wholly wasted, and I am happy to report that he went on to become a very good player indeed to whom I have lost many a half crown.

In common with a great many people I put my clubs away on September 3, 1939, and did not expect to touch them again until the war would be finished and tranquility restored.

Just before Christmas, however, a relative announced that he was coming home from the South for a brief break and couldn't we have a game. He was, and still is, an eager beaver, and therefore it behoved me to get into some sort of shape against renewing our jousts.

I cadged a game at Crow Wood with a friend, I being then temporarily in limbo, as it were, between leaving one club and joining another.

The day we chose was gurly and grey, the course was sodden after days of rain, and the greens were no better and no worse than inland greens usually are in midwinter. And I never played better in my life. Even with two penalty strokes for the one wild drive I hit—ah, happy days—I was still round in the low 60's, unbelievable but true.

The explanation of unexpected excellence after a lay-off is not too difficult to find. When we play regularly we have our quota of bad shots every round. It is the bad shots we remember.

I think that the bad shots get ingrained in our subconscious when we are playing a lot, and only a longish period of abstinence can expunge the recollection of such bad shots. So when we set out again after having played no golf for months, even years, we are so delighted at the prospect of playing again that we have forgotten our fears, we have forgotten our shibboleths. "There's a ball, let's hit it" is all that's in our minds.

We should try to be as philosophical as Bobby Jones, who never hit a ball after his operation in 1948. When he engaged a new secretary in 1956 he told her, "I haven't played golf in eight years; but, then, I haven't missed a putt either."

Scratch with Daisies (1973)

Sir Alexander King, who died last week full of years and honours and achievement, had a passion for golf and a pretty wit.

He never missed the Open championship when it was in Scotland and had a wonderful time last year at Muirfield. He was looking forward to this year's championship at Troon and will be greatly missed, not least by the American players, whom he knew well.

He will be missed even more at Nairn, which he loved this side of idolatry and where his devotion to the course and the game will be remembered each year when the King Cup is played for.

It was at Nairn that I got to know him well, and many a round on the putting green we had. During one of those exercises I asked him what his current handicap was. "I'm playing to a 10 now, but I'm scratch with daisies."

I suppose that remark dates both him and me. If he had said it to a younger man, he might have received the bewildered reply: "Scratch with what?", for selective weed-killers have long since banished the daisy from our fairways.

No longer do young, penniless golfers (if there are any such these days) endure the misery suffered by us old-sters in our youth when a golf ball had to last us until either we lost it or it lost its paint. I can well remember, at Millport and Lundin Links, hitting tee shots smack down a fairway that was precious near as white with daisies as our fairways have recently been white with snow, and spending an unconscionable time, head down, seeking my ball in a sea of white.

Alex King meant, of course, that he was a wonderful

swinger so long as there was no ball to be hit, and who of us has not the same feeling? There is no tension, nothing but well and fair, and we can make the club whistle through the air.

But are we really scratch with daisies? Once I had a salutary reminder that this golfer at least was not. I was an early starter in a tournament at St. Andrews, and a press photographer, seeking a picture for the early editions of the evening papers, was reduced to asking me to give him a practice swing. Flattered, I produced my "scratch with daisies" swing and the picture duly appeared of an exuberant follow-through.

Sometime afterwards I met the late Jack McLean, who asked how my game was. I replied, sorrowfully but truthfully, that my driving was horrible "I thought so," said Jack. "I saw your picture recently. You're hitting from the top." It was an expert diagnosis from what I would have called slender evidence, and it was true into the bargain!

Two Caddies of the North (1973)

How many caddies, I wonder, would go to their grave with among the pall-bearers a former president of the Scottish Golf Union and the captain of the club for whose members they exercised their talents.

Such a one was Callie, who used to carry at Nairn for R. J. R. Gordon and K. M. Cameron, two doughty figures in Northern golf. On a medal day he would carry for one in the morning and, in the afternoon when his other employer took the first tee, he would be promptly told what he had to beat.

"We've got a 72 to beat" was how he would put it, and so long as his master remained in the fight, it was a question of "we" and "us." But should the master falter and fail, the "we" changed to "you," and if the failure were complete enough, Callie would impose the most dreadful strictures, even, when he became thoroughly disgusted, taking out his teeth to give more venom to his imprecations.

When he died last summer, full of years and also, I suspect, full of the product for which Speyside nearby is famous, he was shepherded to his rest by Gordon and Cameron and some others who had enjoyed the benefit of his acid advice. I can't think that any of the caddies at Augusta, however valued, will have Palmer and Nicklaus at their graveside.

There was another old caddie at Nairn, slightly more devious than Callie, who at least was transparently honest in his judgment of his player's performance. He, too, went to his grave last year, and, like Callie, was attended by the high and the mighty of the club.

After the ceremony Gordon and Cameron, who are old

friends and rivals on the course and off it, were discussing the ancient. "He was a cunning old devil," said Ronald Gordon, "but I liked him. He used to drop in to see me from time to time, and he always ended up by saying: 'One thing I liked about you, Ronnie (the easy familiarity was characteristic), you could always handle Kenny Cameron.' Many a 10 bob he got out of me just by saying that."

And, of course, Cameron was able to reply, "Old devil indeed. He used to drop in to see me, and he always ended by saying: 'Well, Kenny, you could aye handle Ronald Gordon', and that was 10 bob from me, too."

The Power of the Irish (1974)

Sean Burke, the Irish amateur golfer who died last week, might never have reached the mature age of 74 but for the magnanimity of a Scottish soldier.

At the time of the troubles in Ireland, Sean Burke, an active young "rebel," as the phrase then had it, was captured by a British Army patrol led by an officer from the South of Scotland. It was at a time when rebels were commonly shot on sight, but the Scot for some reason or other—perhaps Burke's baby-face innocence—allowed the youngster from Lahinch to go free.

Years later the two met again, in happier circumstances, at Hoylake during the first International meeting of all four home countries, although all four did not play one another as is now the practice. Burke, by then the best amateur in Ireland, was, of course, in the Irish side, and his former captor and savior was present as a representative of the Scottish Golf Union. They had a moving reunion during which golf was hardly mentioned.

I recall the episode because, but for the Scot's action, Irish golf, and British golf too, would have been deprived of one of the most exciting sights I for one have ever witnessed—Burke standing on a tee and lashing the ball out of sight. Burke was the forerunner of a whole school of Irish amateurs who individually and collectively hit the ball much farther than any corresponding group from the other countries.

Most of them were big men, but there was one who hit the ball just about as far as anyone else, and he was, as my old grandmother would have put it, just a rickle of bones. He was Dr. J. D. MacCormack, who had been so badly wounded in the First World War that he was patched up with silver plates. He was thin as a lath and looked even thinner because he wore riding breeches on the golf course, but he used a long, heavy driver, slung the club-head back in a full swing, and hit with every ounce of his spare frame.

Burke, by contrast, was big and beefy, though he had a tiny voice and a handshake like a damp dish rag. But he had a glorious swing, round and free, and I have even seen him use a driver out of ragged rough and cart the ball all of 250 yards when a lesser man would have recovered safely onto the fairway.

The Irish reputation for long hitting was not a myth. It was pretty well documented at Portmarnock in 1949 during the International matches when a long-driving competition was held, just the sort of competition I suggested recently should be held at this year's Open. At Portmarnock, James Bruen won with a carry of 280 yards, Joe Carr was second with 265 yards.

There were other Irishmen who loved to have a go. Two of them were R. C. Ewing, from Sligo, and Dr. Billy O'-Sullivan, the King of Killarney. They were alike in that both were big, strong men, and unlike in that they used entirely different methods.

Ewing was well over six feet and built to match, yet in addressing his ball for a drive his heels were only inches apart. He seemed bound to topple on his face, but he secured himself against a fall by having a swing so short you felt he could have swung in a telephone booth. And he squirted the ball miles only a few feet in the air. I know, because I tried to play him on a windy day on his own Rosses Point course and had a terrible time getting within speaking distance of him off the tee.

Dr. Billy, on the other hand, had a wide stance and a round-house swing—but it was a swing with a difference. A visiting American described it this way: "He was worth watching not only because he hit the ball a country mile, and straight, but also because of his unique method of attacking it. The split second before he unfurled his back-swing, he widened his stance by moving his right foot about eight inches farther to the right. This step back, he believed, was the secret of his power, since it widened the arc of his swing appreciably, but, while everyone agreed with the soundness of his theory, no one switched over to the O'Sullivan method."

The Cruelty of Sport (1975)

Long before I had heard of Thomas Carlyle and his essay on "Heroes and Hero-worship," I had my own private collection of heroes, all from the world of sport. The first was Joe Beckett, a heavy-weight boxer who for a time was touted as the Great White Hope, and I can still remember the dismay and childish agony I experienced when Beckett was knocked out by Georges Carpentier. It was not the fact that he lost the fight: it was the incredible fact that he was knocked out in 72 seconds. Total eclipse without all hope of day. Beckett was, in a manner of speaking, never heard of again.

He came into my mind this week when I learned of the death of James Wallace, the Troon Portland golfer who had a crowded hour of glorious golf lasting a whole week which ended, incredibly and unfairly, in total eclipse. And of Wallace, too, it could almost be said that he was never heard of again although he lived to his allotted span and was for many years a valued and much-liked club professional.

There is something especially cruel about sport, infinitely more cruel than the world of politics or commerce. No one can believe, for example, that Mr. Heath will not rise again from the ashes of defeat in the Tory leadership struggle, though that defeat was humbling. But who, to change from one arena to another, remembers Frank Haffey, who once kept the Celtic goal so secure that he was chosen to play for Scotland and then, one black afternoon at Wembley, gave up nine goals and thus won a most invidious place in the chronicles of soccer football. He, too, was never the same man again.

Jim Wallace, however, will always occupy a special

place in my sympathies. I knew him well, having played against him in a Scottish championship when, for once, his sound putting deserted him. He was a stuffy golfer, effective rather than elegant, with a notably closed stance in contrast to another Troon amateur, Bob Garson, whose stance was so open as to defy the textbooks. But both had the great facility of keeping the ball in play, of being content to let their opponents make mistakes.

Wallace, I said, suffered unfairly in losing the final of our Amateur championship at Prestwick in 1934 by 14 up and 13 to play—the biggest margin ever recorded in the history of a championship that goes back nearly a century. He had played so well all week and beaten so many good players, including five men who had played in the Walker Cup match a week or so earlier, that he did not deserve to be destroyed in his last joust.

Lawson Little, his conqueror, had a much easier passage to the final. True, he had beaten Eric McRuvie, from our Walker Cup side; the great Irish golfer, Lionel Munn; and Gordon Peters, then on the threshold of a notable career. But Wallace beat the American, Chandler Egan, in his first match, and then Cyril Tolley, Eric Fiddian, and the incomparable Jack McLean before he met and beat a very formidable American, George T. Dunlap, in the semi-final.

If Wallace could have stopped then, he would have been remembered for a very long time for a wonderful championship record. But, of course, he had to go on, and it was his misfortune that he met one of the great golfers of the century at the peak of his form.

Little was a bulky young man of immense power and wonderful delicacy of touch. He had shown in the Walker Cup match at St. Andrews that he was a man to be feared, for he trounced Tolley by 7 and 6 and won his foursome, with Johnny Goodman, by an even larger margin. But we were not to know, when he took the tee against Wallace, that this was to be the first side of another impregnable quadrilateral, in its own way, almost as impressive as that other quartet of victories achieved four years earlier by Bobby Jones.

Little won at Prestwick, he went home and won his own country's Amateur championship, and bless by soul if he did not do the double again the following year—four Amateur championship victories in a row. Nobody had ever done that before, not even Jones; no one has done it since, and the odds against anyone's ever doing it again must be incalculable.

It would be agreeable to report that I saw every stroke of that sadly memorable final in 1934 between Little and poor Wallace, but truth compels me to admit that I missed the first five holes. It was due to no dereliction on my part but because the start of play was advanced by half an hour to allow the Americans to catch a train, there being no convenient jet service from Prestwick in those days.

By the time I picked up the match on the sixth tee, it was virtually over. Little had gone off like a hare—4 3 3 4 3—and was four up. Nobody could have caught him. It was too late for Jim Wallace.

God Rested—Golfers Did Not (1978)

When I learned last week that, starting at Muirfield in 1980, the final round of the Open championship will be played on a Sunday, it crossed my mind that the Royal and Ancient Club should send a deputation from their Championship Committee to the churchyard at St. Andrews to pay obeisance and make apology at the grave of Old Tom Morris.

It is true that the Open has finished on a Sunday in the not-so-distant past, and at St. Andrews into the bargain. When Jack Nicklaus and the luckless Doug Sanders tied for first place in 1970, the play-off was decided on the Sunday when Nicklaus won by a stroke after driving through the green at the last hole and then stuffing in a putt of about five or six feet.

The putt rabbited into the hole, and Nicklaus was so relieved and delighted that he hurled his putter into the air, a rare display of emotion for this wonderfully composed man. Five years later, at Carnoustie, there was another Sunday play-off, when Tom Watson beat Jack Newton, again on the last green.

But those play-offs were exceptional and necessary because the modern professional operates to such a tight schedule that if the players involved had been required to cool their heels on a golf-less Sabbath there would have been a fine how-do-you-do. I do not suppose any one of them would have followed the ancient example of David Strath in 1876 when he refused to play off after having tied with Bob Martin, but there would have been some hard thoughts and hard words, too.

I mentioned Old Tom because he held very strong views on Sunday golf and possibly his influence is still potent at St. Andrews: to this day there is no Sunday play on the Old Course. Old Tom's shade will be pleased at that, because it was he who insisted that "if the gowfers don't need a rest on the Sabbath, the course does."

Old Tom was, of course, a pillar of the Kirk as well as a paragon of the game. He was once a representative elder from the Presbytery of St. Andrew at the General Assembly and dined at Holyrood House with the Lord High Commissioner, then the Marquis of Tweeddale. One of his companions at the dinner chided Old Tom gently for eating so frugally, only to be told, equally gently, that he had had "a gude denner at the recht time o' day and couldna eat at this time o' nicht."

Sunday is now possibly the day of the week when more golfers are in action than at any other time. It was not ever thus. I am old enough to remember when Sunday golf was regarded as a thought unseemly, especially among those brought up in the Presbyterian tradition as I was.

Indeed, the first time I played golf on a Sunday I was rather ashamed of myself, which was the more discomforting because I played uncommonly well and would have dearly liked to trumpet my triumph.

I felt, in fact, like the Irish priest with a passion for the game who rose very early one Sunday morning to have a few holes before Mass and for the first time in his life had a hole in one. And he had to hug his secret to his own bosom.

There is the most respectable tradition in Scotland of playing golf on Sunday going back to ancient times. Nearly 400 years ago there were records of golfers being charged with playing on Saturday "in time of fast and preaching" at St. Andrews, at Perth, at Leith, at Stirling, at Cullen, and at Banff. The offence, however, was not the playing of golf but of going to golf instead of going to church. Walking about the streets in sermon time was as much a breach of kirk law as playing golf.

James I and VI, who has been dubbed "the wisest fool in Christendom," was not so daft in his appreciation of the situation. "When," he asked, "shall the common people have leave to exercise if not upon the Sundays and holidays (holy days), seeing they must apply their labour and win their living in all working days?"

Maybe some modern ministers had the wise king in mind when they decided to bring forward the time of their Sunday services to an earlier hour in the hope that the golfers in their congregations would achieve the best of both worlds. This was certainly not the thinking of the Championship Committee of the R. and A. in deciding to make Sunday a playing day at the Open championship from 1980 onwards. Their thinking was strictly commercial—a victory for Mammon and defeat for Old Tom.

The Man Who Beat Bobby Jones (1978)

It must be difficult for today's generation of golfers to appreciate the impact of one match in the Amateur championship more than 50 years ago. That was the match in which the 21-year-old Andrew Jamieson, of Pollok, beat Bobby Jones in the fifth round at Muirfield in 1926, and beat him handsomely by 4 and 3.

In so doing Jamieson created a legend which endured until the day of his death last week. All his life he had to bear the burden of being known as "the man who beat Bobby Jones." It was a burden that he bore with grace and modesty, although there must have been many times when it proved tiresome.

No amateur golfer today could create such a legend, principally because there is no one in golf today who carries the aura and authority of Jones in 1926. True, that was before Jones had won his greatest triumphs, but he was already a legend. He was, at the age of 24, the undisputed greatest golfer then living. He did not win his first major championship until 1923, but when he did begin to win he seemed incapable of stopping—or of being stopped.

He won the U.S. Open in 1923, he was second the following year, and lost a play-off for the title in 1925. He had won the U.S. Amateur in 1924 and 1925 and was, inevitably, expected to win the Amateur championship at Muirfield when he came over with the U.S. Walker Cup team in 1926.

Jones had immense prestige, immense authority, but, wonder of wonders, a little-known Glasgow golfer with a smooth swing, an educated putter, and a quietly cheerful temperament took him firmly by the scruff of the neck—a stiff neck, by the way—and beat him handsomely with excellent golf.

Whether the result would have been different if Jones had been fully fit is what might be called a great perhaps. Jones made no excuses. "A golf match," he wrote, "cannot be postponed like a boxing match until both contestants are fit for competition. It is the player's business to come to the tournament not only in proper practice in so far as his golf is concerned, but also in proper physical condition. If I had failed in either respect, it was the fault of no one but myself. I would go out and do the best I could, so long as I could lift the club at all . . . Jamieson played a beautiful round of golf, so much as was needed to beat me 4 and 3 . . . It was certainly no discredit and no accident to be beaten by a player of his ability."

Oddly, it was not Jones's long game that let him down—he putted badly and time and again could not hole the two-yarders that his fine approach play left him. Jamieson kept his head, had a little bit of luck at the thirteenth when a hooked tee-shot bounced kindly off a bank on to the green, and never allowed himself to become afraid of winning.

Jamieson could not follow up his signal success by reaching the final. He was ahead in the semi-final and then wilted, understandably enough after the exertions, physical and mental, of the morning.

But he had done enough for enduring glory and that his victory over Jones was no fluke he proved the following week at St. Andrews in the Walker Cup match. He and Cyril Tolley were handled roughly by Jones and a fellow-Georgian, Watts Gunn, in the foursomes, possibly because the lordly English giant and the quiet young Glasgow man were not very compatible partners, but Jamieson handsomely won his singles match against Bob Gardner and thus fully justified his selection.

Jamieson had a notable career in amateur golf for many

years after his annus mirabilis. The very next year he won the Scottish title at Western Gailes, beating in the final the Rev. David Rutherford, a parish minister from Biggar. He was runner-up in the championship four years later at Prestwick to Jack Wilson.

His great strength lay in his short game. He was a beautiful putter with, ironically enough, a club very similar to the one that his greatest opponent made famous as Calamity Jane. He was so deadly with this implement, which he used to twirl in his fingers as he was taking his stance, that I, in my innocence the first time I played him, thought the club was responsible rather than the player.

When he putted me off the course at Western Gailes, I left determined to get a putter like his—and I did, too,— but I soon learned that the magic rested in the man, not the club. Still, my conversion to Jamieson's kind of putter has lasted more than half a century and today, out of respect and admiration, I'll give it a twirl in my fingers as I face my first putt.

Jamieson, as an unwitting agent of a fate far larger than any he could have imagined, was responsible for a crucial forward step in Jones's fabled career. It had been Jones's intention to go home immediately after the Walker Cup match, but his failure in the Amateur championship made him change his mind and wait over for the Open at Lytham.

In the result, he played the two famous qualifying rounds at Sunningdale, one of which, the 66, was rated to be as nearly perfect as had ever been accomplished—33 out, 33 home, 33 shots, 33 putts. And then he went on to win the Open, his first British title, at Lytham. In the process he played the famous shot at the seventeenth hole from a shallow bunker over 170 yards of scrub and sand hills to the heart of the green that virtually won him the title.

The Tory and Willie Peacock (1979)

A few years ago I gave some advice to an earnest civil servant who had recently succumbed to the blandishments of this infuriating game as an escape from involvement in high affairs of State and the eccentricities and demands of his political masters.

"What," he asked me, "is the secret of playing good golf?"

There was no single secret I said, and I even so far forgot myself as to dredge out of my memory a Latin tag which I thought might appeal to an Oxbridge double first, "Quot homines, tot sententiae." "Ah, yes," he nodded, "so many men, so many opinions. But surely Terence did not play golf."

Finally, we settled on what the great James Braid once laid down—that the most important thing any golfer should remember was to keep the head steady. "I'll remember that," said my acquaintance and, goodness, he must have.

Not long ago I met his wife, a comely consort, and asked her how her husband was finding life under the Tories. She was uncharacteristically and even distressingly vague about her husband's work but not at all vague about his golf when I rather timidly asked how he had fared since last I saw him.

"Terrific," she glowed. "He plays every Saturday and every Sunday. I never see him."

I made the usual sympathetic noises only to be pulled up gently but triumphantly, "He's getting on splendidly. He has won the last four tournaments at the club."

How exactly has he accomplished so much in such a relatively short time? He is not a natural athlete and has no special qualities apart from a first-class brain, that might help to set him apart from other golfers.

Maybe he was intelligent enough to be able to do what the great Willie Peacock did. Willie was probably the greatest water-polo player Scotland has ever produced. He was good enough to play for Britain in the Olympic Games in Paris, that same Olympic Games in which Eric Liddell won the 400 metres after refusing, because of his religious scruples, to compete in the 100-metre heats because they were run on a Sunday.

Peacock numbered among his opponents the mighty Johnny ("Tarzan") Weissmuller, who did terrible things to the Scot under water and to whom Peacock did even more terrible things in turn.

Well, when Peacock hung up his swimming trunks he took up golf and decided that he had better sit at the feet of the masters. This he literally did, for on the first day of that Open championship at Prestwick which Jim Barnes won when the crowd overwhelmed Macdonald Smith, Peacock was on the first tee when the first player drove off.

He saw everyone drive, he saw everyone play a brassie shot, an iron shot, a pitch, a bunker shot if possible, and a putt. At the end of nine hours' continuous watching he broke his fast with hot pies and beer to sustain his massive frame.

Within a year or two he was down to single figures and was a very formidable player.

I am sure my civil servant has prepared himself for golf in nothing like so heroic a fashion, but he has done it and done it well. I salute him, tipping my cap on a steady head.

PART III

PLACES

The Red Badge of Caution (1960)

It came as an agreeable surprise to me at the week-end to encounter in practical form what I had hitherto known only as an old precept in the famous 1890 Badminton Library volume on golf.

Towards the end of the chapter on "Etiquette and Behaviour" there is this quaint passage which I had thought to be now hopelessly outdated in this bustling modern age when all the world golfs, and golf courses and the players thereon are part of the accepted order of society.

"On some links," it is laid down in the Badminton book, "it is especially requested, as a means of warning the public of the approach of danger, that the golfers should wear red coats." And with my own eyes on Saturday, peering through the murk at Wimbledon (golfing, not tennis, variety), I saw just such dangers to the public appropriately arrayed.

Members of the Wimbledon Common Golf Club are required to wear, if not exactly red coats, red jerseys, red cardigans, or red wind-cheaters. If you are not a member and seek to play there, you must equip yourself, by borrowing or by hire, with what I think, paraphrasing Stephen Crane, may be called the red badge of caution.

Thus you conform with that further precept in the passage the beginning of which I have already quoted—"It is but fair towards the local members of the club whose guest or visiting member you temporarily are that you should array yourself for the nonce in the uniform of the danger signal. Otherwise any damage inflicted on the unwary passer-by by your approach unheralded save by the hard flying golf ball will be laid at the innocent door of the club, to the injury, in the opinion of the vulgar, of its local habitués."

The Wimbledon Common course in this "Scotch Corner" of England is laid out on common land, to which everyone has access. The golfers are tolerated, but the price they pay for the privilege of playing is that they must be properly dressed. And to ensure that they conform, bowler-hatted rangers riding ponies patrol the common and discipline the non-conformists.

The rangers must have had an easy day on Saturday, for it was not even a day for a dog to be out—and there are usually, I am prepared to believe, more dogs and their owners than golfers on the common. But it is certainly a pleasing thought that an old tradition is preserved on a course with its roots deep in the history of the game in England.

In my own golfing lifetime, which spans rather more than half the gap in years between the appearance of the Badminton book and the appearance on the first tee at Wimbledon Common on Saturday of three red-coated players, I have seen red coats worn at courses where no such condition of membership was laid down.

At Millport in the early 'twenties, at least one sturdy traditionalist invariably wore a red blazer on the course. At Barnton, the home of the venerable Royal Burgess Golfing Society, I saw a red-coated member eating his luncheon as late as 1938. For all I know, the tradition may endure to this day—and a very good thing, too.

To be sure, there are many clubs where the red-coat custom does persist, but only to the extent that the captain and past-captains wear hunting pink tail coats at the club dinner and when the captain is representing his club at the dinners of kindred clubs. No doubt it is outmoded, and certainly expensive for the captain, but it seems to me a desirable link with the past, and as an unrepentant *laudator temporis acti* I am thankful.

It seems to me good, too, that golf clubs should have their own tie and that the members should, whenever possible, wear their tie when at their club. This is especially desirable when the tie is not just a meaningless arrangement of stripes or symbols but bears some significant connection with the history of the club. The tie of the Royal and Ancient Golf Club bears the silver cross of St. Andrew; the Royal Wimbledon club (near neighbour of the Wimbledon Common club) bears in red on a blue ground the windmill which is part of Wimbledon history.

It is not to be expected that every time a club member knots his club tie he is aware of a feeling of tradition and continuity, but he can hardly escape at least a sense of community with other wearers, and what is a club, any club, but a community? If it is not, then the founders of all the thousands of golf clubs throughout the world were wasting their time.

A Rough Island Story (1961)

Details were seemingly hard to come by, as though there were a conspiracy of silence. "The few survivors of those responsible for the visit," wrote my correspondent, "are inclined to be cagey and, unless I'm mistaken, a wee bit touchy about the affair." Baldy Craig of a newspaper called *The Glack*, for example, who was the Machrie Golf Club secretary at the time, gets a faraway look in his eyes when the subject is broached, dismisses it as: 'Oh aye, it would be some time about 1936,' and diverts the conversation to more realistic channels like the price of beasts or the state of the root crops.

So I had to get the assistance of a newspaper friend to look it up in their files. He reported that on August 10, 1937, Hagen and Kirkwood played over Machrie's 9-hole course, when 200 spectators were present. No scores are given other than that Hagen did the second round in 30.

Here I should insert the results of my own investigations of the origins of this famous occasion in the golfing history of Arran Island. Hagen, I have been told, was persuaded by a Scottish friend in America before he made what turned out to be his last visit to Scotland that he should certainly play at Machrie during his tour. The American-Scot, it is alleged, meant the Machrie Hotel Golf Club on the island of Islay, which is one of the truly noble courses of Scotland though it is known to comparatively few because of its remoteness. Machrie on Arran Island has far far fewer claims to distinction as a test of golf, but it was to Machrie in Arran that the great men were directed. My correspondent now takes up the story:

"It was a perfect afternoon. The Kintyre hills were purple, the Kilbrannan Sound was that beautiful shade of blue just darker than the sky, and the Machrie course was lush, of which latter amenity the sheep and cows were taking full advantage. Fences, of course, kept these animals from soiling the greens, but did not prevent the rabbits from happily skipping around and making little scrapes.

"The *Herald* says 200 spectators, but this I do know—the Machrie boys were expecting a crowd, for every able-bodied local from the laird down through the social scale of farmer, grieve, ploughman, orraman, to halflin seemed to be sporting a steward's badge.

"It was to this scene, then, that the golfing entourage arrived, consisting of one 1925 vintage 4-door saloon boiling after its effort over the String. Hagen got out and surveyed the bucolic scene. He turned his head heavenwards as though looking for, or maybe hoping for, a cloudburst. Kirkwood's reaction was more stoical. It may have been that the general rusticity of venue brought back memories of the Australian Outback and made him a little homesick. After all, there was little to choose between us gawping locals and a bunch of aboriginals.

"Their opponents, local lads, each had a highly individual style—one was a wiggler, the other a cross-hander. After the locals had played off the first tee Hagen first of all mimicked the wiggler and then Kirkwood put his left hand below his right and had a go—not a very good one if I remember rightly.

"The local wiggler used to stand straight up and rigid, all rigid, at the address. Then the rapid wiggle would start and would not cease until he had reached a comfortable sitting position before releasing the power blow. It was this style upon which Hagen based his clowning act, and in retrospect his action seemed rather cruel and uncalled for."

Still, I have it on other evidence that Hagen was charitable, too, on that occasion. One of the local lads produced a new ball for his first drive and was just on the point of striking when Hagen stepped forward and, in the kindliest manner, suggested that he might get on better if he took the paper off.

For the record, as the modern jargon has it, the wiggler and the cross-hander were one up after nine holes. "That," says my correspondent in conclusion, "is fact. I remember the excited conjecture at the interval about the ultimate result. Would it have been headline material had it turned out other than it actually did, 3 and 1 for Hagen and Kirkwood?"

That was one game I should dearly like to have seen. I should also have relished hearing Hagen's remark on the second tee, when a toad louped over his ball and he stepped back to survey the scene—"Guess there's a helluva lot of stooards around here to-day, Joe."

He was a great man, and I am sure he bore no ill will to anyone, unless he and Kirkwood were on a percentage of the gate.

"This for Scotland" (1965)

There cannot be a golfer of quality who has not sustained himself during a dreary practice exercise by pretending before each stroke, or at least before each holable putt, "This for the Open Championship."

It is an amiable and harmless fantasy. None of us, with the possible exception of three golfers in Scotland, is ever going to find himself in that position. In fact, we do well if once in every so many years we find ourselves on the last green grovelling over a four-foot putt, and suddenly realising that we have in fact, "This for the medal."

And that's enough to turn our knees into jelly, to glaze our eyes, and to convert into a coal-heaver's clutch what was before the moment of truth a sensitive arrangement of the hands that even Vardon would have approved. As the charwoman mumbled into her gin, "It's me nerves, ducky."

The best players, I suppose, are those with the best control of their nerves, and the greatest demands are made upon them on public occasions of high importance. Thus any of us is capable of holing a long steal in a moment of bravado on the last green to save or win the Sunday morning half-crown. Would we be equally capable, say, on the Tom Morris green at St. Andrews on a summer evening when there is inevitably a bank of critical onlookers?

Sometimes the hour brings forth the man, and not only on the golf course. A few days after Scotland's humiliation by Wales in a Rugby game at Murrayfield I met a Rugby aficionado who assured me in tones solemn enough to warrant a greater occasion that for the first time in 40 years he was not going to use his tickets for the game at Twickenham. He was disgusted with some of the Scots performances. "Players," he mourned, "used to die for their country. Now they don't seem even to try."

Golf does not provide such moments of high drama as Rugby and soccer if only because the pace of events is slower. But some golfers have been capable, under the spur of playing for their country, of moments of achievement that cannot wholly be explained by technical excellence.

There was, for example, the very long putt that H. G. Bentley holed on the seventeenth green at St. Andrews in the afternoon of the Walker Cup foursomes in the *annus mirabilis* of 1938. That putt, coming when it did, assured Britain of a halved match and enabled us to face the morrow with a slender lead on which, eventually, a noble victory was constructed.

Now Bentley was a fine putter with a superb nerve. Was it not he who, in the semifinal of a French championship, was faced with a huge putt on the last green to keep the match alive and, after settling himself for the stroke, straightened his back and enunciated in his best Lancashire French, "Tres difficilé"? He then put his head down again, holed the putt, won at the extra hole, and went on to win the final.

There was no such light relief on the Road Hole green. It was all nerve and skill and patriotic endeavour. The occasion produced the performer, and Bentley was a great performer under stress. The thought of defeat never entered his head.

Once I played against him in an international foursome at Hoylake. My partner was Jock Smith, himself a great fighter when, as he put it, "the smell o' battle's in ma nostrils." Bentley's mate was Eric Fiddian and a rare fight we had.

We were one up going to the twelfth, at which point an English onlooker asked Bentley how the game was standing. "Oh," he replied jauntily, "we're one down—just now." And he made good the boast implicit in his reply, for he knocked in a stiff putt near the end of the game and we finished all even.

This quality of stuffiness, of refusal even to contemplate defeat, is more to be valued than an immaculate swing or any other technical accomplishment. It was a quality possessed to a rare degree by Freddie Tait, who was a wonderful match-player and always at his best when playing an Englishman, especially if that Englishman was Harold Hilton. He always made mincemeat of Hilton and, what is more, enjoyed the operation. As Bernard Darwin put it, "Freddie took perhaps some unchristian pleasure in crushing him."

Once they were to meet in the fourth round of the Amateur championship on Hilton's own Hoylake. Hilton was the Open champion and clearly the match was one for the connoisseurs. Tait was seen practising putting at lunchtime and was asked, "Is it going well?" "It will be this afternoon" was the ringing reply, and it did.

Tait, you see, was not playing for himself alone when he played someone like Hilton at Hoylake. He was playing for Scotland, and if he gave a thought to anything when he was practising his putts it was not "This for the Open championship," but "This for Scotland and the overthrow of Hilton."

The Road Hole (1966)

The last time I played at St. Andrews, in the autumn medal, I was having a good day with my driver, so good, in fact, that when I reached the seventeenth tee I blithely despatched my tee-shot smack over the sheds to the middle of the fairway.

There and then the thought struck me that this might be the last time I would play just such a stroke, for British Railways have the notion to build a hotel more or less where the black sheds rear their formidable cliff to intimidate the craven or incompetent.

Maybe it was the thought of such iconoclastic intent that made me take three putts on that slippery shelf of prepared turf that lies between the little bunker and the paved road, though that is perhaps to lay too much blame on an organisation that so easily lends itself to criticism.

If the sheds go, the Road Hole will never be the same again. In the olden days, before the railway was taken into the heart of the town, the line from the station at Leuchars ended more or less where the sheds now are, and the hazard used to be the stationmaster's garden, not, as now, a coal-ree (shack).

The sheds, when first I played the hole in the early 'twenties, were used by a local clubmaker for drying hickory shafts and had not, I have been told, anything to do with the railway. Well, there are no shafts to dry now in this age of steel, but the sheds are still there—and I would like to think they will remain.

True, St. Andrews is badly in need of hotel accommodations. British Railways should, I suppose, be commended for their enterprise in seeking to make good part of the loss, though why anyone should want to go to St.

Andrews by train, unless by sleeper from the South, I find it difficult to understand.

There is, admittedly, a wonderful feeling about getting out of the express at Leuchars station to pick up the little local train and hearing the porters turning up their words at the end, and there is still a thrill in chugging over the Eden estuary and catching the first glimpse of that improbable but inimitable terrain that is the Old Course, with the outline of the old grey town in the distance.

Before you have had time to get your bag down from the rack, you're rolling past the sixteenth hole, with the Principal's Nose and Deacon Sime only a wedge shot from your carriage, and with a rush you're beyond the seventeenth tee and into your haven.

That's the romantic bit of the train journey, but it's an uncommonly long time in coming if you have travelled from Glasgow or Edinburgh, and it's altogether easier and immeasurably quicker to go by car, even by bus. Still, every golfer once in his lifetime should go to St. Andrews by train, and, if at the end of his journey, British Railways has a hotel to cosset him in, so much the better. But I could wish the hotel were not where the sheds stand.

Tee It High in a Gale (1966)

Even the best golfers, perhaps because they are the best, dislike practising in the wind. Only last week Michael Bonallack, the English captain, wisely forbade his players to practise at Royal Porthcawl in Wales on the day before the international matches began because the wind was too fierce.

Maybe he remembered a moment at the Masters when he and Ben Hogan were side by side on the practice ground. It was an almost perfect day with only a flicker of wind disturbing the tall pines that fringed the practice area. Hogan played scores of shots with all his iron clubs but only a handful of shots with his driver. "I never practise driving in a wind," he explained, "especially a wind coming over my left shoulder."

I remembered that comment a month or so later when I found myself at Nairn on the day before the annual golf week began. I had arranged to play with a local lion of the North, who suggested that if the great professionals, Dai Rees and Max Faulkner, had arrived by the time we were scheduled to play we would "take them on," in his confident phrase. There was a great wind coming in from the west. It was too great for the professionals. "Play in a wind like that?" said Dai, with undertones of Eliza Doolittle. "I wouldn't play in a wind like that for all the whisky on Speyside," said Max, "but, if you insist on playing, tee your ball high all the time."

The lion and I went out alone. I teed the ball high even into the gale, and drove like Palmer.

A Proper Pace (1966)

Not long ago I was playing in a monthly medal with two agreeable and accomplished fellow-competitors. It was a pleasant day, our golf was no worse than it might have been, and we had reached that stage in the round when the thought of a long, cool drink was a not-too-distant prospect.

Then the peace of the morning was shattered. One of the three players following us requested, peremptorily it seemed to me, that they be allowed to go through. They were "waiting for every shot" and, as an afterthought, "we are being pressed from behind."

Now, this had never happened to me before, and I was somewhat nonplussed. For a moment I thought to answer flippantly, or even rudely, for we had not, I swear, been dilatory. To be sure, there was a clear hole in front of us, but there were two singles ahead and that was in the natural order of things.

I swallowed my pride, my rage, and my sense of the comic and gravely indicated that the request would be granted forthwith. We holed out on the next green and settled down to await the overtakers. And then something delicious happened that not even in my most uncharitable mood could I have stage-managed.

One of the golfers behind us lost his ball near the green of the short hole we had just completed. We waited, they searched. My companions were all for continuing, but my blood was up by now and I insisted we observe the rigour of the game. Eventually the man who made the original request to go through was exasperated enough to shout, "Oh, you had better play on," but I retorted acidly that he had created the situation and he could live with it.

Alas for his luckless friend, the ball remained lost, and eventually, with a very ill grace, the man in a hurry growled a request that we play on. We did, and by some miracle all three of us pounded the ball far and sure and we never saw our pursuers again.

With such an experience fresh in my angry memory, I had a deal of sympathy for Cobie Legrange, who was last week adjured to speed up his play in the Senior Service tournament at Gosforth Park. He must have felt as did Jack Nicklaus when the great American was put under the whip in this year's U.S. Open championship. Nicklaus is, of course, notoriously slow, so slow that after he won our "Open" at Muirfield in July one commentator said with truth that the "Golden Bear" was in danger of becoming the "Golden Bore."

By contrast with Nicklaus, one of the greatest golfers of all time was also one of the most decisive and certainly one of the swiftest. Gene Sarazen, given a clear field, would go round almost any championship course in two and a half hours and be among the leaders. He may have dropped the odd shot by playing too quickly, but who is to say he did not save even more by not brooding?

For my own part, I can recall a game I once played at Killermont with the late Willie Doleman, who was for so long match secretary of the Glasgow Club and a wonderful little golfer with the most perfect economy of effort. We played a match one morning, and we completed the round in five minutes under two hours. We finished all square, both having played as well as we knew how. The play-off was a more leisurely affair—we took the full two hours.

The Links of Gore and Glory (1966)

When the Celtic soccer team won the European Cup last week in Nantes, France, my thoughts went back down the years to boyhood golf at Millport.

The Celtics played their game at the Malakoff Stadium, an improbable name for a football arena in France, though any student of the Crimean War will readily offer an explanation.

In that war Britain and France fought side by side, and one of their hardest tasks was to subdue the fortress of Sevastopol. The siege was finally lifted when the French, under Bosquet, stormed the Malakoff redoubt, one of the several forts encircling Sevastopol.

It was a day of bloody battle, that eighteenth day of September, 1855. No fewer than 19 generals fell, and I can only assume that Nantes had some connection with the victorious forces and commemorated their gallantry in the name of the local football stadium.

Where, then, does Millport form a link with Nantes and the Crimea? Well, what used to be the second hole at Millport was called the Malakoff. It was for me, as a boy, rather more than a full drive over a rocky ridge to a green guarded by yet another ridge, and possibly the lay of the land bore some resemblance to the configuration of the Sevastopol redoubt.

The first Millport course was not built until more than 30 years after the Crimean War ended, and the Malakoff was the third hole of the original layout. Again the assumption must be that the architect, or whoever named the holes, had either fought in the war or at least knew the lie of the Sevastopol land.

At least one golfer I know of was actually at Sevastopol.

He was William Doleman, in his day one of the greatest of amateurs. As a young man he served in the Royal Navy at the Siege of Sevastopol, but it was many years after that before he became a famous golfer.

He was nearly 50 by the time the Amateur championship was instituted in 1885, but he played in it with distinction until he was 74. I remember his son, who was for many years match secretary of the Glasgow Club, telling me that his father's eyesight by then was so bad that he had to use field-glasses to pick out the flag on the green, and then he played his shot, as it were, from memory.

I would like to think that it was he who named the Malakoff at Millport. For all I know he may also have named the Redan at North Berwick, one of the most famous of all short holes and, like the Malakoff, named after one of the forts at Sevastopol.

So distinctive is the Redan, which means a V-shape presenting a salient angle to expected attack, that the great American architect, C. B. Macdonald, put a Redan on almost all the courses he designed, the most famous being the Redan at the National Golf Links in Southampton, New York. And I just hope that there are some historically minded Americans who, failing to catch the fourth green at the National, assuage their sorrow by remembering their link with history.

There was, for a time, a disposition to name golf holes after famous battles. Machrihanish goes one better than Millport or North Berwick in drawing on not one war but two. It has one hole called Balaclava (the Crimea) and another called Rorke's Drift (the Zulu War).

There are many Spion Kops on golf courses, which take their name from that mountain in Natal near Ladysmith where Sir Redvers Buller and the British suffered a defeat from the Boers that caused much heartburning as well as grievous loss. Spion Kon, which means Look-out Hill, was also the name of a Derby winner, but that's another sport and another story.

There is one other famous battle commemorated in the name of a golf hole, though doubtless there are others that my more literate readers will recall. The seventh at Troon, that most perfect of drive-and-pitch holes, is called Tel-el-Kebir after the battle in 1882 when Sir Garnet Wolseley defeated the Egyptians in a Suez campaign rather more successful than the one 10 years ago.

That was only four years after Troon had been instituted, which makes the choice of name much more understandable than Millport's Malakoff 30 years later or North Berwick's Redan, for golf had been played at North Berwick for many years before the Crimea was ever heard of.

The only other link with history that I can readily remember as being part of a golf course is to be found at St. Andrews. If you hook your drive to the ninth hole on the Old Course, you are likely to find your ball hard against the steep face of a long, narrow bunker. It is called Mrs. Kruger, and if she was as forbidding as the bunker that bears her name no wonder Mr. Kruger was such a stern enemy to the British in the Boer War in South Africa at the turn of the century. He himself gives his name to the two bunkers in mid-fairway that catch the mildly errant drive to the right on the same hole, but it is his wife who can literally destroy your day.

Grace Notes at Gailes (1967)

For many months now two members of Western Gailes have played there almost every Saturday, sometimes in medal competitions, more often in singles together or in the friendly four-ball. Each time their clubs have been borne by a pair of boys, who are not only keen caddies but ardent golfers.

They have contributed greatly to the friends' enjoyment, so much so that one day this summer they decided to reward their young assistants with something more than their customary Saturday *douceur*.

They took the boys to one of the municipal courses at Troon, played a round with them, shared with them what the late Willie McCulloch called a "sumpetuous repast," and then delivered them by car to their family hearth and home.

A good caddie is a joy to have at one's side, a bad one is a misery. We can penalise the bad one, but how rarely do we have the wit to reward the good one other than with money.

In my time I have had my share of good caddies and also of bad ones. The good ones were not always those who could club me to nicety. Rather were they the ones whose nature was sympathetic, who knew in their hearts even if they were no Latinists the truth of the Roman dictum that "There's a time to speak and a time to be silent."

Gene Sarazen tells a famous story about the best and wisest of all caddies, old Skip Daniels, who steered him to triumph in the Open championship at Deal in 1932. Sarazen led after two rounds with 139, three strokes better than Percy Alliss, four better than Charlie Whitcombe, and five better than Archie Compston.

Sarazen began the make-or-break third round with three cast-iron pars, and then after a grand drive at the fourth, "I hit my approach off the socket. Daniels did not give me a second to brood. 'I don't think we'll need that club again, sir,' he said matter-of-factly." The rest is history.

I was never in a position to deserve such philosophic nurturing, but once I did have a caddie who went to extraordinary lengths to ensure my success. It was during an Amateur championship at Muirfield and my opponent was taking me very firmly by the scruff of the neck.

I could do little right, he could do little wrong, and on the ninth tee I was four down. There I hit a poor drive and, in disgust, turned to my caddie who, instead of following the flight of the ball, was closely studying something in his hand which he plunged into his pocket when he saw my sour eye light upon him.

On being challenged he said, "It's a field mouse, sir, I'm keeping it for luck." For luck, forsooth. I made him release it, and with it went the luck, the bad luck that had plagued me for half the round. I came home like a roaring lion and won on the last green.

In the next round I picked up another caddie, a mere boy, whose master had in a manner of speaking joined the great golfing majority in the morning. He was a splendid little fellow whose home was in Tranent, bright and cheerful but not too ebullient. We got on famously until, oddly, the same ninth tee, where he had a violent nosebleed which was staunched only by his using up all the hand towels I was carrying against the possibility of another kind of deluge.

He survived, so did I, and next morning he turned up bright and cheerful and early, with all the towels freshly washed and laundered by his mother.

I must be thankful for not having had the caddie who attended a golfer of some eminence in a competition on an Irish course. This eminent person found himself faced with an approach shot which he reckoned needed a 7 iron. "It's ounly an 8" said the caddie, and they argued for a minute or two. The player, in order to cool his temper and reinforce his own judgment, walked forward some 25 yards to survey the terrain. He looked back at his ball, and there was the caddie in the very act of playing a perfect shot to the heart of the green. He stormed back to be told, with a triumphant air: "Oi tould you—it's ounly an 8."

A Tale of Spirited Play (1967)

I know of a course in the Midlands of England where more than one player has the agreeable habit of carrying in his ball pocket a bottle of brandy. It remains inviolate until someone, anyone, has a birdie, and then out it comes for all the players to have a swig.

If either my partner or I had had the wit to be so fortified on last Sunday, the day before Christmas, we might not have survived the round, for our more deadly opponent threw birdies at us from the very first hole. We would have had immediate solace, but the bottle would have been the first casualty. No doubt we would have enjoyed a hilarious Christmas eve.

Only the other day I learned of a match that was played, literally, in the most spirited fashion. It was played on a course, which I know well but which must be nameless, by three players whom I knew by name though only one of them by repute.

He was a formidable player, the combative type who, if he had found himself playing in the Open with Palmer as his fellow-competitor, might well have challenged the great man to play for a £1 sidestake—and this at a time when he was probably earning at most £5 a week.

One night in his cups he accepted, rashly it appeared, a challenge from two useful six-handicap men to play their better ball for £5 each. His liability was, therefore, £10 or two weeks' wages—a sizable sum but quite within his capacity to win in normal conditions. But the conditions imposed were not at all normal.

He had to drink one quarter gill of whisky, neat, on each tee, beginning at the first. He was brave and combative, but he was also prudent. He consulted his doctor,

who in turn consulted the local chemist, who suggested
that the player drink a pint of olive oil just before the
game.

On the day of battle the three players gathered on the
first tee, with two camp followers. One carried the whisky
bottle and an imperial measure, the other carried the single player's clubs.

He had already downed the pint of olive oil and he took
his first "nip" on the first tee before smacking a beauty
down the middle.

The player beat his two opponents handsomely by 6
and 4 and was three under 4s when he finished. A par
finish would have given him 68 (if he could have survived
four more "nips"), and that was just about what he used
to accomplish on his good days.

His caddie took him home after the game, apparently
stone cold sober, but next day he could not be wakened
and slept until three in the afternoon. He woke with the
father and mother of all headaches, but probably consoled
himself with the reflection that £10 will buy an awful lot of
aspirins.

Now this seems to me to be a remarkable tale of endur-
ance. If my reckoning is right, he drank, in the course of
about two hours, three-and-a-half gills of whisky, neat,
which is nearly three-quarters of a bottle. To be sure he
was taking fairly vigorous exercise, he walked about three
miles up hill and down, and he had the benefit of a sea
breeze to keep him awake and alert.

His caddie, I should have added, was also his doctor.

Watching and Suffering (1969)

One of the great and moving stories of golf concerns the seventeenth hole at Prestwick as it was played in the final of the 1899 Amateur championship by John Ball and Freddie Tait.

The big Alps bunker was flooded, and Tait played a miraculous shot out of a deep puddle onto the green, to be followed there by Ball, who played an equally great shot from hard, wet sand close under the face of the black wooden sleepers.

Tait's ball was a gutty, and floated, and it rocked on the little waves he made in the puddle as he waded in, like Agag, who, as every student of the Bible knows, walked delicately.

It was while the ball was rocking and Tait was taking his stance that a Scottish supporter of the gallant Black Watch officer was heard to cry out in agony, "Wait till it settles, Freddie, wait till it settles."

There are moments in every sport and in many spectacles when one's emotions are over-wrung.

Take, for example, the old gentleman F. L. Lucas describes in his essay on Tragedy who, in the middle of "Othello," stood up and thundered, "You great fool, can't you see it's all right?" There could be no truer tribute to Shakespeare and the actors.

It is the onlooker, not the participant, who suffers most, and who enjoys the most exquisite joy from a superb *coup de main* or *coup de theatre*. Thus, one of the most moving moments I have seen on a golf course was while Hogan was playing the last hole at Carnoustie in that memorable 1953 Open championship.

He was, humanly speaking, home and dry after his

drive, which was immensely long and plumb in the middle of the fairway. No doubt he was seething with emotion, but he looked like the little ice man as he stalked stiff-legged down the deserted fairway from which all but the players and their attendants had been banished.

There was a vast crowd all willing him on to victory, but no one, I swear, was more involved and more interested than some of his fellow-competitors playing behind him. They paid him the greatest tribute any golfer can win, for they postponed playing their own shots at the adjacent sixteenth and seventeenth holes and stood, almost reverentially, watching as he settled down to the shot and then drilled a perfect medium iron into the heart of the green. And they clapped, too, like the rest of us.

The only really great golfer I know who wears his heart on the sleeve of his jersey as openly as any of his admirers is Palmer. Goodness, how he suffers when he plays a bad shot! The head cocks to the side, the great hands clutching the club twitch it in the air as though to swing the ball back to safety, and then the downcast look of perplexity moves the hardest heart.

This, of course, is why he is so much admired. We can identify with him. He scowls when we scowl, grins when we grin, and contorts both face and figure when a long putt rims the hole. No wonder his army shrieks and groans—and I assure you, in America these are no figures of speech. His supporters had to be prepared for anything, and he had a fine flow of lurid language to greet the wayward shot. When I saw Duncan play as a tiny boy, I was on one occasion the only person who followed him after he had sliced miles off the line. He turned to me with a voice like thunder and said, "Well, son, what do you think of this bloody game? I hope you play football," and did not wait to hear my hero-worshipping, stammered avowal that golf was my game.

I should dearly have liked to see him play a characteristic round at Nairn with a local caddie who used to be servitor of a great friend of my own. This caddie knew the agony and the ecstasy of his master's golf. He identified with the player so closely that he upbraided him in public for a bad shot in language that would have scorched the whins like a flame-thrower and when he got really angry at what he thought was his employer's obtuseness or plain stupidity, he took out his dentures to give greater force to his strictures!

Jones and the Amateur Spirit (1969)

Bobby Jones was 67 yesterday, St. Patrick's Day, and I hope all good Irishmen, and all men of good will everywhere, sent up a little prayer for him.

It is no secret that this man, who in his day bestrode the links of the world like a Colossus, is now living on borrowed time.

His competitive instinct endures—and there never was a greater competitor when he was pitting his talents against the best in the world. He was an amateur golfer who matched and mastered the professionals at their own game, and his record is in the books for all to see.

He ceased to be an amateur, in a technical sense, when in 1930 he gave up tournament play and made a series of instructional golf films. But he has remained an amateur at heart although, ironically, he is in the main responsible for promoting the greatest professional tournament in the world.

The 33rd Masters Tournament at Augusta will be held next month under, it must be hoped, Jones's aegis once again. He and a New York investment banker, Clifford Roberts, were the men who began the tournament, developed it and the course where it is played, and in the process of time have established standards of play, promotion, and general conduct of a major event that have had a profound effect on golf and golfers in the United States.

The Masters is, to the onlooker from abroad, a combination of Ascot and a Buckingham Palace garden party. It is a great spectacle, a social occasion, and also a parade of golfing behaviour and good manners, to say nothing of golfing excellence, unequalled in the world of golf.

Jones and Roberts say, modestly, that "we would like, if we can, to contribute something to the advancement of the game," and if one may judge from the letters written by prominent competitors, admittedly winners who have reason to feel good about the tournament, they have succeeded.

Thus Palmer says: "There will never be another tournament to equal it," and that was after he had won two Masters with two victories still to come. Nicklaus says: "The tournament was run with the dignity and perfection that will never be topped in the game of golf"; Player insists: "The Masters is the best run of any tournament in any part of the world."

Now all this has not happened by accident. Clearly it came about because the only begetters had certain principles which they were determined to maintain, and something of a clue to these principles was given in a statement made a few months ago by Jones at a time when the American professionals—tournament players and less glamorous members of their association—were at bitter odds over the future conduct of their affairs.

"There seems to be little appreciation today," said the great elder statesman of the game, "that golf is an amateur game, developed and supported by those who love to play it.

"Amateurs have built the great golf courses where the playing professionals play for so much money; amateurs maintain the clubs and public links organizations that provide jobs for the working professionals; amateurs spend millions of dollars each year on golf equipment and clothing; and amateurs rule and administer the game on both sides of the Atlantic.

"In this way golf has prospered for several centuries. It would appear to be the best possible arrangement.

"In the current controversy the tournament players apparently are choosing to regard themselves only as performers whose skills are to be sold to the highest bidder. They have a great box-office appeal in person and on television, and so earn magnificent incomes in these days of free spending and fat advertising budgets. Even so, they obviously feel they could get more money under a different set-up.

"This is certainly within the rights of the players, but it would seem that they are risking two things: first, they may price themselves out of the market and, secondly, they may disrupt the P.G.A.

"The millions who play golf at country clubs and public links are the amateurs to whom I have referred. It is they who support the game, and the tour and the professional golfers. There is no indication that the tournament players have any great concern for the multitude."

From Prestwick to Hilton Head (1970)

Hilton Head Island, off the coast of South Carolina at Harbour Town, was named after its discoverer, one Captain William Hilton. A golfing tradition has endured in South Carolina for almost as long as in Scotland. At the close of the eighteenth century golf clubs definitely existed in both Savannah and Charleston where Scottish settlers had brought the game. From 1788 on, says "The Story of American Golf," "the Charleston *City Gazette* carried notices of the South Carolina Golf Club, in the main reminders to the members of club anniversaries.

"Some anniversary meetings were held on Harleston Green, where a putting green may have been maintained, but there is not so much as a word to indicate that golf was played and none of the implements has been discovered."

As late as 1811, however, according to an invitation that has been preserved, "the honour of Miss Eliza Johnston's Company" was requested "to a Ball to be given by the Golf Club of this city" (Savannah), but war broke out in 1812 and thereafter references to golf in South Carolina die out.

Pete Dye was therefore operating in an aura of tradition when he and Nicklaus laid out their course on Hilton Head, and it was appropriate that one of the most striking features of the course has been derived from a Scottish links that is steeped in tradition.

Anyone who has played Prestwick for the first time must have been struck by—and indeed he may well have himself struck—the sleepered faces of the three famous bunkers. These are the vast Cardinal at the third, the almost equally vast Himalayas (fifth), and the Alps (seventeenth).

The faces of these bunkers are shored up with old railway sleepers, originally to prevent erosion of the sandy soil, and the sleepers have played their part in golfing history. Only a week or so ago I was recalling the recovery shot played by John Ball from wet sand under the sleeper face at the Alps after Freddie Tait had played from casual water in the same bunker. And there is the tale of James Braid at the Cardinal which still sends sympathetic shivers down my spine.

"It was in this very same bunker," wrote Bernard Darwin, "that his supporters saw with horror the great Braid trying to throw away the championship in 1908 by playing a game of racquets against those ominous black boards."

Probably no one who has played Prestwick a few times has not had his moment of horror when a "thin" shot banged into the sleepers and ricocheted into the Pow Burn or some other evil place.

Dye was apparently impressed by Prestwick's sleepers. The thirteenth green at Harbour Town is guarded on either side by two 'pit traps,' as Dye calls them, each as deep as a man is tall. The sides against the green have been banked with boards off an abandoned barn. At Prestwick this artificial banking was done as an erosion measure. At Harbour Town it is simply for effect, but a startlingly atmospheric one.

The other idea borrowed from Prestwick is that of having "wastelands"—oversized bunkers of sand and dirt left permanently unraked, all because Dye was impressed by the size of the Cardinal bunker at Prestwick, which is so huge that it seems to have no beginning or end.

So, at two of the holes on the Harbour Town course at Hilton Head he has these "wastelands," and one of them,

130 yards long, has an old lifeboat in the middle of it, half-submerged as though to warn you what can happen to your round if you find yourself marooned.

"Should Ah Know You?" (1970)

A few weeks ago I renewed acquaintance on a social occasion with a Very Important Person in affairs of State with whom I once played a memorable round at Gullane No. 1.

He has been, in his day, a player of quality, the best of foursomes partners, as I know from his record, and the stuffiest of opponents, as I recall from that game at Gullane. He asked kindly after my game, which I found difficult to defend, and when I asked after his, he replied with a terse "Rotten."

It was, I suppose, some sort of catharsis for a civil servant who must guard his every public utterance with care to be so forthright, and we then indulged in something of an orgy of self-reproach and mutual commiseration that we had fallen so low in our own esteem.

We are nearly of an age, our friends tell us that we still have reasonably good swings, and yet we suffer from the same complaint: we cannot drive. He, poor soul, plays such golf as affairs of State allow him on East Lothian courses where bad driving is penal, and I have Killermont's trees to punish me.

Happily we turned the conversation to the game we had played 10 years ago at Gullane in company with a tycoon and a Very Eminent Person from one of the newer Ministries, and my friend recalled an episode on the first tee that I had all but forgotten.

Caddies, as we all know, are a vanishing race, but so eminent was the man from the Ministry that our host, the tycoon, roped in one of the few remaining ancients of the links for his service. The rest of us, tycoon included, had our caddie carts.

When the caddie arrived I recognised him immediately—a black-avised (swarthy, sunburnt, probably unshaven) little man of infinite wisdom who had carried for me at Muirfield and St. Andrews in the late 1920s and early 1930s, some 30 years before we met again on the first tee at Gullane.

I greeted him warmly, to be met with a suspicious "Should Ah know you?"

"You ought to," I replied, "you took me to the last eight of the Scottish Amateur at Muirfield."

"Whit would your name be?" he asked. I told him, "My God, Sam, ye've changed," he exclaimed, and a welcoming smile split his grimy face.

The rest was wonderful. He had eyes only for my play, the Very Eminent man from the Ministry was virtually ignored, and in the result I found myself subjected to pressures that I was ill able to sustain.

For example, at the first short hole at Gullane, the fourth, I think, I was first to play and in some doubt as to choice of club. So I asked, of everyone in general, no one in particular, "A 6 iron, eh?", and the little ancient snorted, "It's only a 7 for you—at least, it used to be." So a 7 it had to be and, *mirabile dictu*, I hit it on the button right up to the flag.

I could do with that little man right now to restore my self-respect and faith in my own game, but he, alas, now carries in the Elysian Fields—or maybe he is fishing errant balls from the River Styx.

There's nothing like a good caddie for giving you a guid conceit o' yourself. One of my closest friends whom I have dubbed the Lion of the North, because he was for long pre-eminent on his course in Nairn, recently encountered one who had carried for him in his days of triumph and who had guided him, scolded him, and sustained him in many hard matches. It was this caddie, as I have described before, who in moments of anguish and dismay at his employer's temporary ineptitude, used to take out his teeth to give more venom to his strictures.

All that, however, was forgotten when they met recently at the end of the local tournament which they used to win every other year. The old caddie had run his eye over the semi-finalists, and when my friend, his erstwhile employer, asked what he thought of the new generation, he spat contemptuously and replied: "Ach, we could have put any wan o' them in oor weskit pocket."

These Visions Splendid (1970)

A non-golfing friend sent me, recently, a photograph taken from Canada Hill on the Island of Bute in the Firth of Clyde, which is just north of the famous golfing links of Prestwick and Troon on Scotland's West Coast.

What gave significance to the photograph was not the golfers on one of the greens of The Rothesay course in the foregound but the distant scene.

In the background were the peaks of Arran, the glittering Firth of Clyde, a scene of total enchantment. If either of the anonymous golfers in the photograph had a nodding acquaintance with Wordsworth he might have said of himself as he walked off the green:

> And by this vision splendid
> Is on his way attended.

The Rothesay course is not, to my recollection of the only game I ever played there many years ago, one of the great courses of the world, or even of the smaller world of Scotland. There are even other clubs on the Firth of Clyde that would not list it in the first three in the area for excellence or difficulty. But it must rank very high for the beauty of the views to be obtained therefrom.

For myself, I claim that Millport on the small Island of Great Cumbrae wins the prize among the courses of the Clyde, but I am prejudiced about the place where I learned much of my golf half a century ago. As a boy I played there with a retired sea captain who knew every ship that came up or went down the Firth to or from the port at Glasgow, and you could see them when they were still a long way off.

To the north, from the highest holes on the course, you

can see up to the Tail o' the Bank and Argyll's Bowling Green, to the south you can see beyond the Wee Cumbrae and over the Garroch Head to the passage between the south end of Bute and the Cock of Arran.

That distant scene had its other advantages. You could see the rain approaching from afar, and as you grew older and wiser in the ways of the weather you could calculate to a nicety whether you had time to play another hole before the squall struck. If there is a prettier sight in the world than the re-emerging distant Clyde scene after a cold front has gone through, taking its sharp showers with it, it has not come before these wondering eyes.

I know that Gourock and Greenock, Helensburgh and Cowal, Routenburn and Kelburn, even the sidehill slopes of Skelmorlie, all have their claims to present the fairest view from their fairways, but I must be allowed the illusions of youth and cleave to Millport.

The Ayrshire coast is only a little way behind the Firth of Clyde for enchantment. From Bogside to Ballantrae the golfer whose game has gone sour can restore his spirits by gazing at the Arran outline, while at Turnberry, there is the bonus of Ailsa Craig and even, on a clear day, the Antrim coast of Ireland.

There are, of course, golfers with no soul for scenery. They are like the over-enthusiastic onlooker watching a great match at St. Andrews before the days of crowd control who replied to the exhortations of a sweating steward—Players, please!—with the understandable but inelegant, "To hell with the players! I came to see the golf."

But there is more to golf than knocking a little ball from point A to point B. That is one reason why Carnoustie and Balgownie and the other fine courses on the East Coast have their limitations. There is nothing to look at except the North Sea. St. Andrews offers the wonderful bay and the view over to Angus, to say nothing of the ancient townscape that lies before the eye on the road home.

Muirfield has its view of the hills of Fife, to say nothing of romantic Archerfield Wood, the Graden Sea Wood of Stevenson's "Pavilion on the Links." And North Berwick has the Bass Rock to delight the eye. Who knows, the black-browed albatross that visited there in recent years might swoop overhead while doing the seabird equivalent of circuits and bumps.

Then there are some of the scenic joys of the inland courses that linger in the remembering eye—Lanark with the prospect of Tinto before us, Boat of Garten where we play in the shadow of the Cairngorms, Grantown with the Cromdale Hills and the Cairngorms always for company.

For the fairest distant scene I return in memory to two old favourites, Nairn and Golspie, with always at the back of my mind Machrihanish and its views of Islay and the Paps of Jura, and Dornoch, golden in the early summer, purple in autumn, with the hills of Sutherland looming on the near horizon beyond the glittering waters of Embo Bay. There is one hole at Golspie, the short 16th, which is called Cairngorm. Right behind the flag, a mere matter of 65 miles away, lies Ben Macdhui, and even if you see it only once in a week, and then only if the weather is fair, it is worth waiting for.

At Nairn, fairest of all the Moray Firth links, the drive to the first hole should be aimed at the left hand of the Five Sisters of Kintail, some 75 miles away. To be sure, you don't need such a marker—the hole is a straightway par 4 with every inch of the fairway visible to the feeblest eye— but what golfer has so little romance in his soul that he would not choose to take his line from a mountain on the other side of the country!

L for Ladies (1970)

A friend of mine who went to see the Masters tournament at Augusta in April had an experience there that was both awesome and delightful.

The week before the tournament began, and before the masters had arrived en masse, he took himself to the vast practice ground one afternoon to work on his game, which is good enough to make him greatly feared in his northern parish.

After he had been pounding out drives all of 230 yards (and that's a pretty long drive for an amateur) he became aware that he was sharing the practice arena with another player. To his dismay—and delight—he realised the other player was none other than the great Jack Nicklaus, who was firing drives right to the limit of the area, which is about 300 yards long.

My friend, with a true sense of occasion, stopped to watch, at which point Charlie Yates, a great amateur and one of the key figures at the Masters, appeared and introduced the two men to each other. Nicklaus was greatly interested to learn that my friend's wooden clubs were hand-made by his local professional, an artist at the bench, and asked if he might see the driver. My proud friend handed it over and was taken aback when Nicklaus, after a minatory waggle, commented: "It's heavy."

Now my friend is no Hercules, rather does he play clubs that I could use, yet here was one of the giants of the game, one of the strongest men in the business, implicitly criticising his key club on the grounds that it was too heavy.

However, Nicklaus asked to be allowed to play a few shots with this "heavy" driver, and proceeded to knock the ball just as far as he did with his own. My friend was delighted, but confessed that, the next time he played, every tee shot went in the direction of long off and he wondered, wryly, if Nicklaus had knocked his clubhead askew.

I was relating this tale to John Panton at Turnberry last week, he being also a friend of the visitor to Augusta, and he commented: "No wonder Jack thought the club heavy. His own driver is less than 13 oz. and it has a super-stiff shaft." Such a club must feel like a knitting needle, with no head-feel at all, which makes it all the more remarkable that Nicklaus can swing so slowly and smoothly.

It seems, however, that he is not alone in using clubs that are comparatively light. Panton himself uses a driver that is only 12¾ oz.—he told me the swing weight but I am a child in these matters—and he added that Hogan also used light clubs, especially his irons, which were not much heavier than standard ladies'.

The best pitching club I ever had was a double-duty I picked up in a pro shop in North Carolina. I liked it from the moment I hefted it and took a divot out of the pro's linoleum, and I had played several rounds and brought many pitches up like a spitting cat before I saw the "L" stamped on its back. Well, if it's good enough for the ladies and for the likes of Nicklaus, I'll keep it.

Death on the Links (1971)

Two friends of mine, eminent golfers both and wonderful competitors, were having a match at Fleet, the course of the North Hants club.

It was a devil of a match, with the slightly less accomplished player one up as they approached the seventeenth green, which both reached with their second shots. As they were walking towards the green the couple in front drove from the eighteenth tee nearby, and one of the players, after driving, slipped, fell, and broke his leg with a crack like a well-hit iron shot.

The more sensitive of my friends, who was, incidentally, the one-up man, immediately suggested to his opponent that they should abandon their game and make for the clubhouse as quickly as possible to summon aid to the stricken golfer.

"Not at all," said his opponent, "we'll hole out. After all, I'm one down." And hole out they did for a half. What is more, they drove to the last hole, the luckless man lying groaning the while, and played the hole with deadly seriousness, even to the extent of measuring their short putts to see who was "away."

Some sort of justice was done when my sensitive friend followed his opponent in from five feet for a halved hole and victory—and then, but only then, they scampered to the clubhouse telephone.

That story had always seemed to me the last word in dedication to the game to the exclusion of outside influences however unlikely and bizarre—until I heard not one but two gruesome stories of ghoulish behaviour on Scottish courses.

In one a friend of mine was the innocent witness of a

tragic happening that intruded on his golf game. He was playing with an eminent personage in one of our nation- alised public undertakings on a South of Scotland course that had better be nameless. They are hustlers on the links—not in the American sense of the word—and were racing round with their caddies when they discovered on reaching a certain tee four golfers whom they had not seen before in mid-fairway just about the distance of a good drive.

They fumed momentarily and were then relieved to be given a "come-on" wave from one of the four in front. They drove, and my friend's ball trundled very near one of the golfers in front who was stretched out on the turf. Judge of my friend's dismay when he learned, on reach- ing his ball, that the man on the grass had collapsed and his companions were waiting for an ambulance. They were members of a vagabond club whose day of enjoy- ment had turned to tragedy.

"What," I asked my friend, "did YOU do?" "I took a No. 4 iron and knocked it right into the heart of the green" was the answer.

But even this pales into insignificance compared with an episode some months ago on a course at the other end of the country from where my iron-nerved friend hit his No. 4 iron. It is a seaside course across which run one or two burns, delightful to look at, diabolical traps for the errant stroke.

Among the members of the club was a rather eccentric ancient who delighted to play by himself in all kinds of weather, with the result that on some days, especially off season, he might be the only golfer on the links.

One day as he crossed a burn at an early hole in the round he saw the figure of a man lying in the water. He gave it no more than a casual glance and continued his round. When he crossed the same burn a couple of hours later at the end of his game the figure was still there.

Again he glanced at it, continued to play, and completed his game. He then went into the clubhouse, went straight to the bar, and told the steward—"I think you should phone the police. There's a body in the burn at the seventeenth. And I'll have my usual."

Perhaps Scots, with their well-known detached attitude to dire accident and death, are different from other golfers. They are like the old Highlander who was leaning on the churchyard wall in a remote village in Wester Ross when an English visitor remarked—"It's very quiet here." "It's a lot quieter doon there," said the oldster, pointing to the graves.

Advice and Gamesmanship (1971)

It's so long since I had a formal lesson from a professional that I find it difficult to remember whether I was told what not to do or what I should try to do. About all I can remember of that lesson, which I gave to myself as a fiftieth birthday present, was that the pro told me to stand farther from the ball. Nor was it a variation of the old jest, "You stand too near the ball—after you have hit it."

I took the lesson to heart, went out to practice the simple doctrine, and played the first nine holes at Nairn in a way that any of the competitors in this month's Northern Open tournament there would gladly accept. The magic did not long endure, alas, but it was good while it lasted, and every so often, when I am in the doldrums, I remember Gregor McIntosh's gruff advice and play above myself for another nine holes or so.

Once before I was given some positive advice from a professional of much wisdom and few words. I was playing a practice round at Killermont with Hector Thomson under the eyes of his father, Archie. We were having a splendid game, nip and tuck, until the fifteenth hole where I hooked a long iron into a bunker. "Too much right hand," I cried in dismay, only to be gently rebuked by Archie: "Too little left hand."

It's the old story of the man with a bottle of whisky—the optimist said it was half-full, the pessimist said it was half-empty. I was the pessimist, Archie the optimist. When I remember this occasion, I recall the advice of the wise Glasgow man who was playing with Harold Wilson at a time when the Labour leader was having trouble with some firebrands in his party: "Keep a good grip of your Left and you'll be right."

Positive thinking need not be quite so peremptory. My favourite fellow-competitor was—nay, still is—a man who once coaxed me round Killermont in a score lower than I had any reason to look for. I happened to hit a goodish drive at the first and he remarked that my swing was just as good as he ever remembered it to be. If I pitched close he averred that I was always a good pitcher, and when I holed an improbable putt he remarked: "You can still use that old thing."

Now that is the very reverse of gamesmanship, which some golfers employ quite unwittingly. It is, as followers of Stephen Potter well know, the art of winning without actually cheating. Thus, I once saw a couple set out from the first tee. One hit a "Monday morning shot"—a fluffy puff into the air—and his opponent avowed with a severe air, "You ducked your right shoulder into that one." He had the game in his pocket from that moment, although he probably was well-meaning in his comment.

Only once—and I lay my hand on heart—only once have I deliberately resorted to gamesmanship. I was playing in a four-ball against a rather tiresome person who was that day the more tiresome because he was driving uncommonly well with a new driver.

He began to be a little patronising when he and his partner were four up just after the turn. "Are you not playing much these days?" he asked me after I had hit one particularly ineffectual shot. Stung, I asked him on the next tee, after he had hit not quite such a booming drive as hitherto, "Is that new driver heavier than your old one?" The rest was easy.

A Square Lunch or Square at Lunch (1971)

It was at Prestwick that I witnessed with my own eyes what I still regard as the most impressive feat of golfing gastronomy that has come within my ken. In 1939 the irrepressible Hamilton McInally met Hector Thomson in the final of the Scottish Amateur championship. They were, if memory serves, square at lunch time, and Thomson ate a simple, prudent meal in what is really a golfing temple of good food.

McInally, lunching with the Prestwick Captain, the great Bobby Maxwell, began with the familiar Prestwick *plat du jour*—mince and poached eggs. He then, at Maxwell's invitation, assailed the cold table with gay abandon. Then gingerbread, still a Prestwick speciality, then biscuits and cheese, and all washed down with a pint of beer—although he was then, on his own admission, a teetotaller who liked to be "sociable."

He skipped only the traditional glass of kummel which seems to be de rigueur with coffee at Prestwick, but he, a non-smoker, had a cigarette, again in the interests of being "sociable." All this, if you please, in between rounds in the final of a championship.

He then went out onto the course and played the first seven holes without a flaw. He won easily against an opponent of the highest class, and to this day I don't know which to admire the more—McInally's play or his performance at the table.

Foursomes at Muirfield (1972)

On a March Saturday I played 36 holes, starting at 10:15
A.M. and finishing at 4:35 P.M., and between rounds had
a leisurely and excellent lunch with civilized preliminaries
and equally civilized post-prandial libations.

Nor was this golfing feast enjoyed at some short course
where one might be expected to scamper round in under
two and a half hours. I played on one of the best and
longest of all courses, Muirfield, and in a match where
every shot was studied with care and played with almost
ferocious determination.

How, then, you may ask, did we manage to do it? The
answer is simple—we played what is known at Muirfield
as a club match, a foursome (true alternate shots) over 36
holes, and I counsel any golfer of sensibility who is wea-
ried of four-ball games or of stern medal rounds to find
himself three companions of equal taste and make his
next outing to the links a 36-hole foursome.

There is one proviso—the match must be on level
terms, with no handicap strokes involved, so you must
choose your kindred spirits with some care so that a gen-
uine match is possible. It might be difficult, for example,
to make a level match if one player is a tiger and the three
others are rabbits. But you can pair a 6-man, say, with a
12-man against two others with handicaps of 8 or 9 and
you can have a devil of a match. Ours finished on the last
green, and if they say, with truth, that any 18-hole game
that goes to the last green is a good one, what can we say
of a 36-hole game that finishes under the wide windows
of the great room at Muirfield?

To be sure, we were inordinately lucky in our weather.
Saturday was a day stolen from June. There was barely a

flicker of wind, the larks were high in the heavens, and you might never, as a visitor, ever again find Muirfield so uniformly balmy.

I certainly pray that come July the professors playing in the Open championship will be put to a sterner test and that the wind will blow sharply, preferably out of the west, to make the first and ninth, to name only two, the great holes they are.

It may also help to explain our rapid progress round the course that we had caddies with a keen nose for a ball hit into trouble, though there was little excuse for the straying shot in the calm air. And the rough has not yet started to grow—nor will it, I am assured, be allowed to become the hayfield it was in 1966 when only the vastly accomplished or the rashly brave used their drivers regularly from the tee. The rough will be graded so that the worse the shot, the greater the penalty, which is as it should be.

Our foursome consisted of the Captain of the Honourable Company of Edinburgh Golfers (the official name of the Club) and this correspondent versus the Recorder and the Chronicler. In brief, we were three up at lunch, one down after 27, two down with two to play, one down with one to play, and we were never really in sight of winning the last hole and were vanquished.

The Cup Twice Lost (1976)

My golfing past caught up with me recently—not once, in fact, but twice in a single day.

I had sallied forth on that most commonplace of errands, to the drugstore only a five-iron shot distant, when I was hailed civilly by a window cleaner with that question which must be peculiar to the West of Scotland—had I the time?

I had, twofold, for after I had told him it was midday he held me in his power like the Ancient Mariner by asking—"How's your game these days?" He had no long grey beard and glittering eye, but he had me spellbound when he went on—"D'ye mind when I lost you the Tennant Cup?"

For a moment I thought the penny had dropped and that he was a caddie who had, in a manner of speaking, lost me my chance of winning that venerably trophy presented to the Glasgow club in 1880 by Sir Charles Tennant, Bt., to mark his captaincy of the previous year.

I had been going strong and when, in my second round, I drove on to the front of the thirteenth green it seemed that I had only—fatal words—to finish in par to win. The pin was at the back of the green, which was then, as now, slightly crowned, and so I made a dutiful journey to the flat to spy the land.

When I returned to my ball I noticed my caddie was holding the flagstick between his feet, and it crossed my mind to ask him to stand to the side and hold it at arm's length in the approved fashion. But it seemed a niggling nicety, especially with a small gallery looking on, and so I stroked a smooth putt dead on line.

There was a gasp from the gallery, my caddie leapt

nimbly to one side, and my ball came to rest where his feet had been—a full eight feet from the hole. Unbeknown to me, while I was walking back to my ball after the preliminary survey, he had removed the flag and stepped two or three yards to the side. It was my own fault, not the caddie's, but when I inevitably missed the putt and thereafter went to pieces, the caddie's conduct was a ready excuse.

So I assumed my window-cleaning friend was the culprit of that far-off day, but I was wrong. According to him, but quite outwith my own recollection, there had been another occasion when I had the winning of the cup in my grasp with only four holes to play and he had persuaded me to use the wrong club to play a tricky little shot from just off the fifteenth green. I have only his word for it, but he was most insistent, going so far as to claim he had been sharply rebuked by the club captain of that time, a supporter of mine. The players in this year's Tennant Cup, which has become a grand affair, will have no caddies. They will have caddy-carts, but who will they blame when they lose?

100 Years and 95 Strokes at Machrihanish (1976)

One of my favourite Punch cartoons was captioned "The One-Note Man." It appeared many years ago and consisted of a sequence of little drawings spread over two, or it may have been four, pages of the magazine.

They portrayed a day in the life of a member of a symphony orchestra leading up to an important concert. The eye followed the player from breakfast through the day until he arrived at the concert hall, through the programme until it reached his great moment, when, in a drawing made in bolder line, he is shown making his distinctive contribution to the evening's music—he strikes one note on his triangle and, replete, retreats into obscurity.

That old-time exercise in irony came into my mind the other day when I was invited to play in a competition at Machrihanish tomorrow to mark the centenary of the club. Perhaps I should phrase it more modestly. There is to be a special competition, and I, as an honorary member, was invited along with many others to take part—and, like the one-note man, to play one stroke.

The competition is described by the convener of the centenary celebrations committee as a multi-person one-ball golf match. The captain of the club, Dr. A. D. Wallace, will drive a ball from the first tee, and that ball will be struck in turn by 90 or so members, including ladies and juniors as well as men, waiting at prearranged points on the course. The ball will be holed out on the eighteenth green by the lady captain and, as the convener says, it should circle the course pretty quickly.

Now this seems to me an admirable way of celebrating a centenary. Of course, there will be a dinner later in the year with distinguished guests and no doubt a routh of oratory and story-telling, but tomorrow's competition will involve a large number of players and there should be splendid fun.

I only hope the weather is not a repeat of the weather exactly 100 years ago. On March 14, 1876, only three days after the club was constituted in the Argyll Arms Hotel, Campbeltown, there was snow and storm. Two days later there was "storm and snow all day," and there was another heavy fall of snow on the 18th. Happily the world is growing warmer and the likelihood of snow tomorrow must be small, but there could be a snell wind coming in from the Atlantic and those players detailed to play their solitary strokes at the far end of the course will hope that the ball does indeed circle the course pretty quickly.

No fewer than 95 players have put their names down to take part and all have been allocated their positions. Even the small boys have been recruited to carry the ball from green to tee where, as between the fourth green and fifth tee, there is a measurable distance of rough ground to be covered.

That should save a second or two, and seconds may count in the end, for there is a sweepstake for a first prize of £20 to the person who guesses the exact time it will take from captain's drive to lady captain's putt.

Times have been allocated at five-second intervals so there may be a deal of excitement round the last green, especially if the convener, J. S. Trappe, has correctly set his snare. One member who is notoriously afflicted by that hell of all golfing diseases, shanking, has bravely offered to play the approach shot to the last after the county champion has driven, so there should be hilarity as well as excitement.

There is some cunning intimidation, too. One player, proud of his excellence with the short irons, has insisted on playing the tee shot to the short fourth, because, he says, he always gets on the green. But Mr. Trappe (how well-named he is) has listed two other players for that hole, "First bunker shot" and "Second bunker shot", a wry vote of no confidence in the player of the teeshot.

No attempt will be made to establish a record for either time or the number of strokes. There is a sort of record for this type of multi-person one-ball match set up a couple of years ago in Australia by 70 players who completed a round of 18 holes in 10 minutes 54 seconds. In America nine holes have been completed in 5 minutes 23 seconds by 34 players and in 5 minutes 14 seconds by 53. But Machrihanish is a stern as well as a beautiful test of golf, March is not the kindest of months for weather, and I do not look to see a total time of much under half an hour.

When it is all over, players and onlookers will assemble in the clubhouse to cut the hundredth anniversary cake and have a drink on the club. And someone, I hope, will remember the lines of the versifier who wrote many years ago:

> Health to each and all,
> The cratur makes us
> clannish.
> Give one good hurrah!
> Hurrah for
> Machrihanish!

Fife Stories (1976)

At last I have found some virtue in one of my pet golfing abominations, the temporary green. It has enabled me to establish a personal record which will never find its way into the archives, but which has given me much selfish, if rather dubious, satisfaction.

The other morning, after early frost, I played a few holes at Killermont.

The greenkeeper, prudent to a fault as it seemed to me, had decreed that some of the flags be located on temporary greens until all the frost had gone. But I blessed him when, at the seventh hole, I played a long pitch and, glory be, the ball finished in the hole for an eagle 2.

That single stroke reduced my eclectic score compiled over nearly 40 years of play over Killermont from 46 to 45. I know there are other old-timers who have done better, and I am also aware that the hole as I played it last week was some 30 yards shorter than the hole as it is usually played, but I propose to hug my little distinction to my golfing bosom even although it was achieved without witnesses.

At least I have spared myself the scathing condemnation that was once visited on a sprightly woman veteran, who was so displeased by an unsatisfactory round that she took herself off to the local professional at the Fife course where she had been a regular player for many years.

The professional was not the most sensitive of mentors, and when she told him she did not seem to be timing her shots right, resulting in a loss of power, he said: "Hit wan or two."

She did, expecting him to say nice things about her

method, but also to see with his gimlet eye where the fault lay. The professional asked her age, and she, with reasonable pride, replied: "Going on 72." "Ach," was the withering rejoinder, "ye're done, woman, ye're done."

Well, I feel I'm not quite done when I can trim my eclectic score, even with the adventitious aid of a temporary green and no witnesses to lay hand on heart and say, "Alone he did it."

Fife professionals and Fife golfers generally have always had a sharp eye and an even sharper tongue.

Ben Hogan's caddie at Carnoustie, Cecil Timms, was such a person. He had many virtues. As Hogan said, "He was a good caddie. He treated my clubs as if they were the crown jewels and kept them clean and shining all the time. He took my shoes home with him every night to polish them." But—and it was a very big but—"When things got tight on the course he would get extremely upset, and the more nervous he became, the more he would talk. Each time I'd stop and quiet him. Many times when I'd have a long putt he'd hold his head down between his arms and wouldn't look, indicating his lack of confidence in my putting. And most of the time I didn't want to look either.

"Timms was never wrong. I don't ask a caddie what club to use, but if I picked a No. 5 iron, for example, and the shot was short, I might comment that I should have taken more club. Every time I did this, Timmy would say, 'Yes. I had me hand on the 4 iron.'"

I once did a radio interview with one of Fife's most famous sons, Willie Auchterlonie, when he was well into his seventies during which he produced a wonderful condemnatory description of modern golf as "just ping-pong," meaning that in his day you had to hit two woods to reach holes that the modern professional, with the steel shaft and a rabbit ball, can reach with a drive and some sort of flip with a pitching club.

Some years later, on the eve of the centenary Open at St. Andrews, I again interviewed him, this time for television. He then produced a memorable phrase when I reminded him that in his long life at St. Andrews he must have known all the great players, including his formidable predecessor as professional to the Royal and Ancient, Andrew Kirkaldy. "Aye," he said, "a rough pebble, yon," and when his words went out over the air they were found displeasing by Kirkaldy's family.

Then there was the other dictum by Auchterlonie that I liked very much. He won the Open in 1893, the last home-based Scot to win the championship, and many years later he was asked by a Glasgow golf writer who had succeeded him as champion. "J. H. Taylor," he said, with respect, "No' a bad gowfer, no' a bad gowfer." And that would be a fine epitaph for anyone who has ever put tacket to turf.

The Truth about Glasgow University (1978)

I was enchanted, when reading an urbane and witty piece by Ian Bowman about Glasgow University called "A Colony in Academe," to find some reference to golf within the precincts of the university when he was a boy living at No. 4, the Quadrangle, when his father, the redoubtable Professor A. A. Bowman, held the chair of Moral Philosophy.

There used to be a field beside the gym—now completely built over—which he said was excellent for practising golf drives. "For pitching with a mashie," however, and the old word dates the period and the player, "the slopes at the front of the university were better, as the ball rolled back to one.

"On one summer evening," writes Bowman, "I was practising pitching when I caught sight of Professor Gloag approaching in the distance. Professor Gloag, who lived next door to us, was Dean of the Faculty of Law, and looked the part. As he sat at his desk, facing the Quadrangle, his high, domed, bald head and staring eyes above a winged collar suggested a judicial presence and made him a formidable figure to the passer-by.

"On this occasion he did not appear to have seen me. I was uncertain how he would react to my pitching and retreated behind one of the bushes. He came down the slope, limping slightly on his stick, and stopped at just about the place where I had been practising. Looking round cautiously, he put his hand in his pocket and drew out a golf ball. He addressed it with his stick, which I now recognised as a mashie-niblick.

"He had a nice swing, and I watched, impressed, as he hit the ball time after time up the slope. When I emerged casually from the bushes, he gave me some useful advice on pitching.''

There has, of course, always been a healthy golfing tradition at Glasgow University. One of my own professors, W. Macneile Dixon, was never happier than when he boarded the train for Prestwick and his regular round. And there never was a more devoted and enthusiastic golfer than Sir Hector Hetherington, who counted a Sunday ill spent if he did not manage a few holes at Killermont after chapel service in the morning. The weather had to be very fierce indeed to keep him and his constant companion of the links, Professor Cappell, in slippered ease at the fireside.

An even more unlikely instance of the assertion that golf is where you find it was brought home to me one winter day about 15 years ago. I had gone for a sort of picnic on the Duke's Road above Aberfoyle and found, near our picnic spot, a golf ball—and not an old battered thing which might have been a dog's toy but one well worth playing. How had it got there, 10 miles, I suppose, from the nearest course? Had it been lifted and then dropped by a gull or crow?

It turned out that the ball had been played by a golfer who had been, like myself on the day I found it, driven from his Saturday round by hard frost but who was determined to keep his hand in. He had his clubs in his car, he spotted some short grass at the roadside, and had practised his pitching. He turned out to be an old friend of my own and, as is the way with old friends, he claimed his ball—and got it.

PART IV

THINGS

When the Golfer Does Not
Eat a Hearty Breakfast (1957)

Any shrewd observer can enter the dining room of a hotel at breakfast during a major golf championship and tell at a glance which of the players eating there are still in the tournament and which are on the sidelines.

The survivors are usually picking at scrambled eggs as though it were a noxious concoction; they toy with toast and gulp great draughts of tea before settling their nerves with a cigarette. The vanquished, or the non-qualifiers, are giving the breakfast the full treatment and for the first time getting their money's worth.

It is all a question of nerves, for, Lloyd Mangrum to the contrary, there are precious few golfers who can eat heartily before setting out on a championship round. Mangrum, who looks like a riverboat gambler and, on and off the course, has all the sinister composure of that trade, insists that professional golf has no more pressure attached to it than any other business. He has gone on record as saying that he does not know a single "pro" on the tournament circuit who is nursing an ulcer.

Now that, I submit, is no more than Mangrum's picturesque way of insisting that he has a better nerve than most tournament golfers. The facts are against him. The most successful British professional of our time, Henry Cotton, had a notorious weak stomach—for food, not for combat. A generation ago Abe Mitchell, also a great competitor, was an equally poor eater and clearly suffered agonies, of the spirit if not of the flesh, when under the pressure of competition. Nearer our own times, Ben Hogan chose his food as carefully as his clubs, and when he won the Open championship at Carnoustie, ate from a packed lunch prepared in the canteen of an American firm in Dundee.

Ideally, of course, the golfer who is burning up his energy on the course should be fortified against the ordeal. But it was a counsel of perfection that Horace Hutchinson laid down more than half a century ago in the Badminton book: "Eat heartily, for you will find your nerve all gone if you try to play golf on an empty stomach."

In thirty years of watching and playing tournament golf, I have only known two men who obeyed Hutchinson's behest. One was Lawson Little, the other Hamilton McInally, and by an odd chance both furnished proof of the excellence of their digestion—and, therefore, of their nerve—at the same course, Prestwick.

In 1934, when Little destroyed Jim Wallace in the final of the Amateur championship by playing unbeatable golf, he had for his breakfast on the morning of the final a large steak plus two fried eggs, toast, marmalade, and coffee. A navvy could not have asked for more, and though Little had a navvy's build, even he must have been nervous at the prospect of winning the British title.

A few years later McInally reached the final of the Scottish Amateur championship at the same Prestwick and finished the morning round against such a formidable opponent as Hector Thomson with all to play for. Now McInally is as jaunty a golfer as ever lived, but even the bravest spirit must have viewed the afternoon round with some disquiet. If McInally was apprehensive, it did not show in his appetite. He ate uncommonly heartily—and Prestwick before the war was a notable clubhouse for the delights of the table. He was then a teetotaller, but he drank a pint of beer "to be sociable." He was a non-smoker, but he carried cigarettes for his friends and smoked one himself—again "to be sociable." McInally then went out and played the first seven holes of the afternoon round as near perfectly as anyone could wish. He won easily in the end, but his real triumph, I am persuaded, was achieved off the course not on it.

Bobby Jones, who knew better than most people the pressures that build up within a tournament golfer, altered his eating habits during his career. I am not sure whether the change coincided with the end of the seven lean years (1916 to 1923), when he was expected to win everything and won virtually nothing, and made possible the remaining seven years when he was expected to win everything and did.

As he puts it in his book "Down the Fairway": "I play better fasting. As a boy I loved to eat; I still love to eat, but not on the days of tournament play. I used to eat plenty of breakfast of my accustomed kind—oatmeal, bacon and eggs, all too frequently cakes or waffles, and coffee. And at luncheon between rounds, hungry from the exercise, I would not think of denying myself something substantial, topped off by pie à la mode. Pie and ice cream—with an afternoon round to play."

And then comes the sad confession, the price of perfection: "Not any more. For breakfast, when I can eat, a strip of bacon and a small chop and a cup of black coffee. For luncheon between rounds a slice of dry toast and a cup of tea."

It is a grim formula for success, but there were some compensations in Jones's case. "I have a good big dinner in my room, prefaced by two good stiff highballs, the first taken in a tub of hot water, the finest relaxing combination I know; and then a few cigarettes, a bit of conversation, and bed at 9 o'clock. And usually I sleep well."

More Than One Way to Hole a Putt (1959)

When the late Macdonald Smith used to make his regular visits to these Islands in search of the Open championship, which he never won (though he was there or thereabouts more often than not), he sometimes stayed in his native Carnoustie to get acclimatised and to practise on seaside turf against the great occasion.

He was, I have been told, a most friendly man behind a slightly forbidding exterior, and nothing delighted him more than an evening round with some of the local amateurs. He was sparing with his advice though generous when that advice was sought, but in one department of the game he was niggardly with his praise. He never applauded a putt unless the ball passed the hole—or dropped in. The most delicate long approach putt laid stone dead was watched in silence if the ball finished only an inch or so short of the hole. If it went a foot past, even three feet past, there was a nasal "Good putt."

Clearly Mac Smith believed that the golden rule of putting was the old axiom, "Never up, never in," probably because in his less successful days he had to fight a personal battle with his own timidity on the green. No one was more daring or deft in playing difficult long irons to tightly guarded greens, but he was not so audacious on the green, and perhaps if he had been less tentative in his putting he might have done better than finish second, equal second, equal third, and fourth in our Open championship. Four more putts holed in three of those championships would have given him victory, and although that can be said of many golfers it was especially true of Mac Smith, who had everything a great golfer should have except the capacity to win when it mattered most.

If, to saunter into fantasy, Bobby Locke had done Mac Smith's putting for him, Smith would not have gone down in history alongside Abe Mitchell as the two greatest golfers who never won the Open championship. And Mitchell, the magnificent striker, the tremendous iron player, the great matchplayer, could not putt under the pressure of pencil and card in the Open.

Of all the great putters there have been in my time, Locke is beyond question the man for my money. Almost any modern professional, with the possible exceptions of Peter Thomson and Eric Brown, would cheerfully, if they were allowed, let Locke do their putting for them, especially in the Open. Yet he would not always have been praised by Macdonald Smith. Locke's talent as a putter consists in his being the safest and shrewdest of players.

If there is danger in being past the hole, he will err, if he errs at all, on the short side. If being short means that he leaves himself a kittle downhill or sidehill putt, he will be bold. He is probably nearer than any of the moderns to Jones, who consistently putted for a dying fall. That is to say, he putted the exact length of the hole and therefore, as he once phrased it, he had four ways of getting into the cup—from in front, from either side, and from the back— with the ball that rimmed the hole gently. Such a method postulates an exquisite touch and judgment of distance which few possess.

Hagen, another wonderful putter, had a different method—or methods—for he was not like the modern players who always strike the ball the same way whatever the conditions or the contours of the green. Hagen would cut a putt into a slope from the right or hook it into a left-hand borrow. He could also be breathtakingly brave on occasion.

At Muirfield in 1929, when a fierce wind swept the links on the final day and glazed the greens, his putting was audacious to a fault. On the twelfth green in the final round, after hitting a shocking second and a bad third that just found the front of the green, he left his approach putt fully eight feet short. Uphill against the wind he banged the eight-footer four feet past and was left with a desperately difficult putt to save himself from taking a seven. Without a tremor he rapped the four-footer into the back of the hole, downhill, downwind and all. Not one golfer in a hundred would have hit the little putt as Hagen did. But then not one golfer in a thousand had Hagen's nerve, and putting, I am convinced, is mainly an affair of nerve.

The most striking tribute I ever heard paid to a man for his putting was during a championship at Prestwick in which Andrew Jamieson was playing. He was, in his day, perhaps the best putter in Scottish golf and, like Jones, whom he once beat fairly and squarely, singularly expert in his judgment of distance. On this occasion he was faced with a four-yard putt for a win at a critical stage in his match, and, naturally he studied the putt with some care. One who knew him well, and had suffered at his hands on the course, was audibly critical of this care. "What's he wasting time for? He knows he's going to hole it." And hole it Jamieson did, right in the centre.

Golf's Sound Barrier (1962)

Sandwiched between Mozart and Stravinsky at 8:55 tonight is a talk by Professor D. G. Christopherson, F. R. S., who from the lofty eminence of the vice-chancellorship of Durham University is to talk for 15 minutes on "The Mathematics of the Golf Swing."

Most of us have, in a manner of speaking, small mathematics and less physics. We are hard put to work out correctly the precise handicap in a tournament when A plays off a 3 handicap, B a 17, and B receives three-quarters of the difference. If Professor Christopherson trots out formulae more complicated than Momentum = MV (mass × velocity) some of us will not be with him for very long.

I would not have it thought that I sneer at the physicists and mathematical engineers. On the contrary, it was a physicist, one of the back-room boys at the Royal Aeronautical Establishment, at Farnborough, who came up with a remarkable discovery under the prodding of the great Lord Brabazon, himself something of an aeronaut (in 1909 he made the first flight in Britain by an Englishman) and also something of a golfer.

This physicist discovered that there is a kind of sound barrier in golf. If you can burst through the barrier you will hit the ball a disproportionately longer distance than a man who just fails to pierce it.

It works this way. A long hitter—which is to say, a good scratch golfer who hits the ball quite far—may work up a clubhead speed of just under 160 feet a second. If he makes a good contact, his ball will carry about 230–240 yards—that is to say, about a yard and a half for every foot per second of clubhead speed at impact. Supposing, however, he can speed up the clubhead to about 170 feet a second, he will achieve a carry of not 255 yards (on the 1½ yd formula) but of 270–280 yards. In other words, the gain in carry is very much greater comparatively than the increase in clubhead speed.

Now these figures I have set down are not to be taken as accurate. They are approximately correct and are given merely to illustrate how the physicist operating modern devices under strict scientific control can help to explain why some golfers hit the ball so very much farther than others. They may also help to explain why on occasion some ordinary golfers hit the ball farther than is their wont. If we do hit a beauty, we usually shrug off the delicious experience by saying, "I timed *that* one right," which is probably an unscientific explanation of a process when, for some reason or other, we whipped the clubhead through much faster than usual, and, since the mass of the clubhead remained constant, the increase in V (velocity) meant an increase in momentum.

Everyone knows how James Braid went to bed one night a short driver and woke up next morning to find himself a very long one. What is not so widely known is that a few hours before short-hitter Braid went to bed he had acquired at a dispersal sale a new driver. Clearly it was the club that transformed Braid overnight because it must have been of exactly the right weight for him.

Those mathematicians who are still with me will realise that with the new club Braid was able to produce an MV product greater than he had been able to produce with his old club. Too light a club won't do, neither will too heavy a club; each golfer has somewhere, not necessarily in his bag, the one driver with which he can hit the ball farther than with any other.

But are the scientists always correct? I wonder if Professor Christopherson has heard the famous story of Professor Tait, who held the Chair of Natural Philosophy at

Edinburgh University in the 1890s. Tait proved to his own satisfaction that a golf ball (the old guttie ball) could not be hit through still air more than 190 yards unless three times the energy were applied. His own son, the redoubtable Freddie, promptly went out on a frosty day at St. Andrews in 1893 and drove a ball 342 yards. The carry was measured accurately by another Tait, W. A. P., a civil engineer, at 245 yards.

78 Nails on His Shoes (1964)

Changing spikes is simplicity itself. A few twists of a key and the job is done—and it's a job worth doing. Every professional agrees that a sound grip is a prerequisite of good golf, and the grip of the shoe on the ground is just as important as the grip of the hands on the club.

They ordered things differently in the old days. Vardon went so far as to include in the illustrations of his book, "The Complete Golfer," the pattern of the nails on his shoes. But his advice reads strangely today.

"Take care that there are plenty of nails on the soles of your boots, and that they are in good condition and the heads not worn away . . . I do not like big nails of any description, nor do I prefer small ones arranged in clusters. Those that I prefer have small round heads about the size of a small pea, and are fluted down the sides.

"I have the soles and heels of my boots freely studded with these, and always according to the same system. There are 25 nails on the sole of each boot and 14 on each heel. . . . There are plenty of nails on the fore part of the sole on which the pivoting is done and where there is the greatest tendency to slip."

No wonder Vardon was well anchored when he took his stance. He was carrying on his feet 78 nails, and even small nails must have weighed a good deal. Vardon at the top of his swing with a full shot was poised on his left toe, with the heel well raised, and it was essential that he should have a firm grip of the turf. Modern golfers barely raise the heel of the left foot.

One American professional, Shelley Mayfield, has stated that "On a full shot with the driver, the left heel is never lifted more than an inch and a half from the

ground." In fact, there are some players, Mayfield among
them, who play all their shots without raising the left heel
at all. They do no more than rock to the right on the inside
of the left foot on the backswing, but on the downswing
they believe in fast footwork and in finishing the full shot
with the right foot poised on the toe.

Hogan was so fascinated by the importance of fast footwork, especially with his right foot, that he used to practise with a golf ball tucked under the outside of his right
foot. That forced him to keep his right knee bent into the
shot even throughout the backswing, and, of course, he
was able to thrust into the shot as soon as he was making
his hit. That is a severe discipline that few of us could
endure, but all of us, I am persuaded, would be none the
worst for following Mayfield's advice not to lift the left
heel in the backswing.

Henry Cotton, who studied every aspect of the game
more thoroughly than any other British golfer, says,
"Shoe-wear is very important, and the thickness of the
sole and general flexibility play an important role in foot
action. I have always liked flexible shoes. I have used
heavy, thick soles but I do not prefer them to the soft
shoe. Correct, fast foot action has always seemed easier if
my shoe bends."

Jones was also a great believer in light-weight, flexible
golf shoes, but his great contemporary, Hagen, was not.
My recollection of Hagen is that his shoes seemed to have
the longest, flattest soles of any golfer I ever saw. He had,
admittedly, very large feet, and they looked larger because he always wore two-tone shoes, that being the fashion in his day. But when he was standing on a tee addressing the ball, his shoes seemed to be gripping the turf
from the tip of the toe to the back of the heel. This helped
Hagen tremendously because he used a lot of footwork,
as might be expected from a golfer who swayed to a
marked degree.

Nobody sways like Hagen now, nobody pirouettes like Vardon. Still, they were not bad players—ten Open championships between them. Styles change; greatness endures.

The Three-Inch Putt (1965)

James Hitchcock won a hole in last week's Honda
match-play tournament when one of his opponents assumed that he had been conceded a three-inch putt and
discovered, to his dismay and his partner's wrath, that
Hitchcock had other ideas.

Hitchcock was, of course, technically correct. Unless he
or his partner, W. Large, had signified concession, it was
up to Jacklin and Caygill to make sure the three-inch tid-
dler was safely put away. Usually, even in cut-throat professional competition, a lifted eyebrow or an interrogatory
"O.K.?" when one ball is inches from the hole wins a nod
of consent.

No such request, silent or spoken, was made at Mere,
and, according to the report, Hitchcock and Large had
turned away after their opponents' ball had died at the
holeside. Their silent departure was assumed to be consent but, as the Highland minister warned his congregation in a cautionary tale, "Ye ken noo."

Hitchcock's opponents went to pieces and lost a game
they might have won, and what makes it worse, Hitchcock and Large went on to win the tournament and collect
£1000 apiece in the process.

I can't help recalling what used to be one of my favourite quotations but which will now always have a rather
sour golfing connotation. "It's an unjust world," said the
Mikado, "and virtue is triumphant only in theatrical performances."

There was something theatrical in Hitchcock's obduracy
but little of virtue, though in this functional and utilitarian
age he can at least claim that the end justified the means.
I prefer the view of one wise commentator who, pointing

out that Hitchcock had right on his side, observed that sometimes the closer one sticks to the letter of the rules, the farther one gets from the spirit.

In all the golf I have played, both friendly and competitive, I have been fortunate in being spared the slightest unpleasantness. No one has ever claimed a hole from me for breach of a rule, and I in turn have never claimed a hole, though once or twice I have been tempted.

The nearest I approached to querying an opponent's conduct was in a championship match at Muirfield. I won at the seventeenth, where my opponent obligingly took two shots in a greenside bunker. After he had played his first shot he smoothed the sand, and at the time I thought this was against the rules. I was, of course, wrong, as he very properly pointed out when, going up the last hole, I asked, in the most diffident way, whether he had in fact broken the rule by his action in the bunker.

In my own defence I must insist that, even if he had won the hole and the match, I would not have disputed the verdict. A man who can't win a golf game through his own merit but has to rely on the wiles of the links lawyer were better to take up bowls.

Gamesmanship is another matter, but only when it is light-hearted and employed for gaiety's sake. It's fun, if you know your company, to suggest to an opponent on the tee of a hole which is within reach of a very long drive, "Come on, Bill, you're the only one with the power to drive this green." And Bill, if he is obliging, will wind one round his neck.

But it is wholly against the spirit of the game to do in earnest what I once did in innocence. I was playing in a dour bounce game at St. Andrews when everything hung on the play of the last two holes. For my second shot to the Road hole I asked my caddie for my brassie, but then changed my mind and took a spoon, with which I laid the ball on the green.

One of my opponents (our partners being out of it) took his brassie and finished through the green on the road. And the half-crown was ours, but only after a rather acrid exchange, for my luckless opponent had not seen me change my club and had assumed that what was the club for me was the club for him.

The Whites of Their Eyes (1967)

Hilton, thou shouldst be living at this hour, England hath need of thee.

The Hilton whom I have arbitrarily canonized was Harold. Wordsworth, who was speaking of Milton, would not mind my changing his M to an H. I cite Hilton because he was one of only two people who have won both the Amateur championship and the British Open championship.

Bobby Jones was the other, and lest there be among my readers those with a sharp memory who think I am not on the Ball, I know that John Ball, eight times Amateur champion, also won the Open championship, but he did it when the competition was decided over 36 holes, whereas Harold Hilton won it not once but twice over the full stretch of 72 holes, and on courses such as Muirfield and Hoylake which were then as now a test of the best.

Hilton, I feel, would not have approved the proposal that the British Amateur championship should be decided by 72 holes of stroke play instead of by the traditional arbitrament of match play. He won the "Amateur" four times and was in three other finals, so he had proved himself at both kinds of tournament play.

Of course, it is probably true that the man playing the best golf would always win over 72 holes, which is not true of a match-play championship, where even the greatest golfer can be caught on the hop by some one having the round of his life.

Joe Carr, who has won the Amateur three times and has also many notable stroke performances in his record, spoke truly when he said that "Stroke play is the purer test of golf but not of character."

It does take character, rather than technical competence, to withstand the unexpected which can arise in a match. You may be comfortably home in two, some eight yards from the hole, during which time your opponent is plowtering along the rough. Then, from nowhere, he holes a long steal, or recovers stone dead out of an evil place, and you immediately begin to wonder whether you can get down in two to get a half.

"Just when you're safest," as another poet put it, there's a bolt from the blue, and then the easiest of shots becomes the hardest, you have to improvise and play the man—and it takes a real man to survive.

Here let me offer a query such as is familiar in quizzes. What have Hamlet, Roper, and Goodman in common? All three met the great Bobby Jones in an early round of a major match-play championship.

The improbably named Hamlet played him in the second round of the Amateur championship at Hoylake in 1921, and so far from playing the game of his life against the American boy wonder, he took 87 to go round Hoylake, but he pushed Jones to the very last green.

Goodman, a stripling from Omaha, beat Jones in the first round of the American championship at Pebble Beach in 1929 when the Atlantan was at the height of his powers, and Sid Roper gave him the fright of his life in the first round of what Jones has called "the most important tournament of my life"—the Amateur at St. Andrews in 1930, the year he won all four major titles.

Roper, it is worth remembering, began with four cast-iron 4s on the Old course and was three down. Jones began 3 4 3, which was devastating enough, and then had the effrontery to hole a long shot from sand at the fourth for a 2. Poor Roper went on doing nothing but 4s until the sixteenth, where he took three putts for a 5 and lost the match.

Now maybe Jones would have played the same kind of golf in a 72 holes stroke-play amateur championship, but no one will convince me that he was not the better man and the greater competitor because he was locked in a cut-and-thrust struggle and could all the time see the whites of his opponent's eyes.

Jones knew what match play was about. "I held a notion," he wrote many years later, "that I could make a pretty fair appraisal of the worth of an opponent simply by speaking to him on the first tee and taking a good measuring look into his eyes. . . . What I observed of Mr. Roper in this respect was not at all reassuring.

"He had a very clear, steady look in his eyes; his manner and his bearing were quite composed, and he had the look not only of a competitor, but of a golfer as well. When he struck his first tee shot, he looked even more like both. . . . I knew right then that I was in for a real game, and how glad I am that I did have this knowledge!"

There is the heart of the matter. Match play is conflict, man against man, and the better man, though perhaps not always the better golfer, will win. Freddie Tait, who was as great a match-player as ever lived and who took a special delight in destroying Harold Hilton in championships and international matches, was right when he said that stroke play was no more exciting than rifle shooting. And he was a soldier.

A Musical Remedy (1967)

When you are getting older and longer, young enough to rejoice in your strength but not old enough to know any better, you can putt like an angel. Watch any boy facing up to an eight-foot putt and you'll see him charge at the hole like Palmer in a victory mood. And, cynically, you murmur—"He'll learn."

When you are getting older and shorter your heart belongs to Hogan, for he is typical of almost all golfers who had a swing in their day but who have lost the art of putting. Hogan can still hit the ball as straight as a laser beam with every club in the bag bar one. When he gets on to the green, he is a sorry sight. The whites of his knuckles proclaim the tension in his hands and heart. In short, as the old Scots caddie might have said, "He can putt nane."

For a year or two now, apart from the odd round, I have putted without much conviction. To be sure, I have never sunk so low as even to contemplate using a croquet putter. I have not even tried to apply Gene Sarazen's gimmick, the "over-40 finger," a method of gripping the putter in which you place the forefinger of the right hand down the side of the shaft.

My putting has been just so-so, but for several rounds in succession in August I putted about as well as any man has a right to expect. What was especially gratifying was that two of my games were played under the normal tension of tough bounce games, when hard-eyed opponents insisted, "We'll see that one in", when you putted or chipped to near-gimme distance.

It all began with a birthday and the gift of a gramophone record which I decline to name lest I betray the loyalty of some too credulous reader. A passage from the record, of a piano concerto, kept running through my head when I was facing up to a putt—a passage of such lovely melody and rhythm that something at least of the rhythm crept into my stroke, and what had been for all too long a scuffling stab became smooth and fluid and, best of all, miraculously effective.

So effective was it that I had only to make a conscious effort to recapture the passage and the long putts went stone dead, the four and five yarders kept nibbling the hole if indeed they didn't drop, and the little ones went in with a Casper plop. It was wonderful while it lasted, but, alas, although the melody lingers on, the song has ended.

Red Lion, Blue Eagle (1967)

Andrew Lang once wrote of Freddie Tait, "I never heard a word said against him, except a solitary complaint that, in the lightness of his heart, he played pibrochs round the drowsy town at the midnight hour."

No one, I am sure, ever said a word against Francis Ouimet except that sometimes, when the occasion was right, in the lightness of HIS heart, he shared in barbershop duets and quartets.

He did it, like everything else he put his hand or heart to, uncommonly well; and it is one of my most cherished recollections that after the Walker Cup dinner in 1934 he and Jack Westland, who later reached the dignified position of U.S. Congressman, sang duets in excellent close harmony to the delight of the entire company.

Francis Ouimet has been in my thoughts this week-end because on Saturday the Troon club, of which he was an honorary member, received from one of its own members a most unusual memento of the quiet American who was one of the great golfers of his time and one of the first gentlemen of the links.

Ouimet was a close friend of the late Archie Fraser, who lived in that most delightful white house that lies between the third fairway at Troon and the sixteenth green. His son, K. D. Fraser, has furnished the memento—the ball, suitably mounted, that Ouimet used to drive himself in as captain of the Royal and Ancient Golf Club in September, 1951.

Ouimet (the name is pronounced weemet, not weemay) was the first, and so far the only, person not of British-nationality to hold that office. It was a very special occasion and, of course, it was a very special ball, prepared in America for the captain's use.

It was American size—recognising the captain's native caution and patriotism—and was probably easier to see and hit at the hangman's hour than our own small ball. It was a special Walker Cup ball, for Francis had been a member, as player or captain, of every American team from the inception of the match in 1922 until 1949.

On one side of the maker's name was the outline of a lion in red, on the other an eagle in blue, and, as I recall the occasion, the captain's drive was everything it should be.

It was, appropriately, a perfect day, with not a whisper of wind, but the air was electric with excitement. The crowd round the first tee was the largest for a captain's inauguration for many years. The congregation of former captains included Viscount Simon, Lord Balfour of Burleigh, Lord Teviot, Bernard Darwin, and two old opponents of the captain-to-be, R. H. Wethered and Cyril Tolley.

A minute or two before eight, the central figures in the ceremony came down the old steps from the clubhouse— the retiring captain, Sir George Cunningham; the captain-elect, bare-headed and bespectacled; and the professional to the R. and A., old Willie Auchterlonie, then 79 but wonderfully erect. He had won the Open in the year that Ouimet was born, 1893, only a few weeks after his twenty-first birthday. He better than anyone else, possibly, appreciated the significance of the feat that first brought the new captain into the world's eye, for Ouimet was only 20 when he won the U.S. Open at Brookline.

As every golfing schoolboy knows, that victory was perhaps the greatest single achievement of any golfer in the history of the game, for this virtually unknown youth not only won his country's greatest title, but in doing so dismissed, in the personal combat of a three-man play-off, the challenge of the greatest golfer then alive, Harry Vardon, and also of Ted Ray, a mountain of a man who had won our Open the year before and who was to win the U.S. Open championship seven years later.

It was almost as though a good Scottish amateur were to beat Nicklaus and Palmer in a 36-hole play-off for next year's Open championship at Carnoustie.

So the atmosphere on that lovely autumn morning at St. Andrews 16 years ago was alive with history. Francis teed his own ball, perhaps to spare old Willie's back muscles; he had only a twitch of a practice swing, and then, with no more sign of anxiety than if he had been driving off on a Sunday morning at Brookline, despatched a perfect drive straight on the railway bridge slightly to the left of the flag.

If the caddie who retrieved the ball had not beaten it down before it stopped bouncing, it would have travelled a full 250 yards, and who can hope to do better than that at St. Andrews whatever the occasion?

There was even something special about the customary caddie's reward. Instead of the traditional sovereign, he received, as I wrote at the time, "no doubt with the consent of the U.S. Secretary of the Treasury and the custodian of Fort Knox, a gold five-dollar piece encased in a plastic frame."

Troon Golf Club, which has its own great traditions, is the right kind of home for the ball used on an occasion that established a new tradition. Francis Ouimet loved Troon, as he loved all golf clubs and courses which had a sense of history.

He made golfing history at least twice, in 1913 and again in 1951. When he died a few months ago, the world of golf was a poorer and less cheerful place.

Pipes and Putting (1968)

The other evening I had a lesson from Gary Player—along with about 100 others. We were watching an instructional film made in South Africa for world consumption, and all of us should be the better, certainly the more intelligent, players for the experience.

Just as Player, a little man, is stuffed with good golf, so is his film stuffed with good sense. It was devoted to trouble shots and the short game, of which he is an acknowledged master, although in a subsequent film of last year's Piccadilly tournament at Wentworth we saw the great man forget to put some of his own precepts into practice.

There were the usual basic rules: keep the head steady; aim behind the ball when recovering from sand near the green or when the ball is lying badly or close to the bunker face; let the clubhead do the work, and so on. But the one hint I tucked into my mind was less instruction than a simple tip.

Player insisted that when you clean your ball on the green, you should always replace the ball with the manufacturer's name perfectly aligned with the line to the center of the cup—that is to say, just above where your putter blade will make contact.

He made the point, very properly, that it is not enough just to look at the ball when you are putting—you must see it—and you are more likely to see it if you have something definite to focus on, viz., the name.

Some pros I know go further. When they replace the ball, they are at great pains to line up the name with the line of the putt, and then concentrate on aiming at precisely right angles to the name.

I suppose if you are playing for crocks of gold every other day every little thing counts, though I have no knowledge that the greatest putters of earlier eras—Locke, or Hagen or Jones, to say nothing of the daddy of them all, Willie Park—resorted to such small stratagems.

Come to think of it, in Park's day the name of the ball was usually inscribed in a circle, so the most he could do, if he thought it necessary at all, would be to set the circle in the Player manner.

At that time, however, the golden rule in golf, which we are inclined to forget in this permissive age, was that the ball shall be played wherever it lies, and it was held to be a sin against the light to handle the ball more than was absolutely necessary.

I knew at least one golfer of some eminence who went a deal farther than Player or the pros who seek to obtain an adventitious aid by lining up the name of the ball on the required direction.

He was a pipe smoker, almost as inveterate a smoker as Ted Ray, who used to play his thumping drives and even more thumping recovery shots with his pipe clenched in his teeth. How Ray did not snap the stem, or break his teeth, or knock the pipe out of his mouth with his left shoulder I shall never know.

He seemed always to be placing himself at risk, or in the position that another friend of mine found himself in on the middle of the fourteenth fairway at St. Andrews. My friend was going well in the R. and A. medal and had hit a fine drive down the Elysian Fields. The second shot was "on" if he hit one of his best, and he laid into his brassie with such a will that he clenched his teeth ferociously at impact and broke his dentures.

To revert to the pipe-smoking friend who, as I said, went one better than Player. Not for him the perils of playing pipe in mouth. He always removed his pipe before every shot, and always he placed it within a few inches of his ball, with the stem lined up on the flag.

He was a notably accurate player, in particular, a splendid putter, and he achieved some modest success in the Amateur Championship, once even beating the great Tolley, also a pipe-smoker but at that time in his cigarette phase.

I don't know if anyone ever challenged this cunning placement of the pipe, for I am persuaded that this was an exercise in gamesmanship before Stephen Potter added that word to the language. It did help him to win games without, I suppose, overtly cheating, but it was stretching things farther than most people would choose to go.

"Sweevel Yir Hinches" (1969)

When Frank Stranahan was at the peak of his power, it was power that brought him to the peak. At least, he was probably the fittest golfer of his era, and almost certainly the only player of quality who included in his impedimenta a barbell and weights that took a strong porter to carry.

In that he resembles many young amateurs of today, all of whom seem to hit the ball infinitely harder than did my generation. They cheerfully take a 9 iron at a short hole where I have never used less than a 7. They get up at long holes with a drive and a big iron where I and others like me have always needed, in the classic phrase, "two guid paps wi' wuid."

Pray, how do they manage to do it? They are stronger, though no bigger, and they are stronger probably because we as a nation have learned a lot about diet and body-building foods that was unknown a generation and more ago.

In the case of my young friend, however, that is only part of the answer. He has recently been doing weight-training exercises at the university that were specially designed by the P.T. staff for the benefit of golfers. They have added, he is convinced, at least 15 yards to his tee-shots.

No doubt it would do me, and others of my age and build, some sort of good if I could discipline myself of a morning to lie supine on the bedroom carpet, hands behind head with a 20lb. disc between head and hands, and raise my tubby trunk a dozen times to a sitting position.

That, they tell me, is one weight-training exercise that greatly strengthens the muscles of both arms and abdomen, and the legs as well. Such muscles have to be in good trim if you are to hit the kind of hefty drive that the P. G. Wodehouse hero exalted above the attractions of womankind.

Alas, truth compels me to admit that although my young friend hit the ball impressive distances, the net result was that he was 15 yards deeper in the rough. As the late Willie Campbell pithily put it, "There's aye a something: if it's no' bugs, the lum reeks."

By a remarkable coincidence my other companion on the day I played with the body-building devotee is another sweet swinger who, like myself, is no longer sylph-like and lissome. He was having a goodish day with his driver, almost every shot going off with a pleasing crack and bang down the middle. But he seemed to have lost some of his distance, which could not be entirely attributed to the deadness of the turf, and when I remarked that he was hitting the ball "very nicely," he insisted that the shots were "all hands and arms. I have no body turn, and it's the body turn that gives you distance."

He was right, of course. No less an authority than Jack Nicklaus supports him. "An especially important factor in distance hitting," says Nicklaus, "is leg strength. Learning to swing by combining a full body turn with a long backswing will help develop the left leg." When the master, like father, says "Turn," we should all turn, but it becomes the more difficult as you grow older.

Palmer says the same thing. "A big turn is a wonderful asset in golf, for the turn generates your power, and the bigger the turn the greater the power." But he goes on to say, no doubt to comfort the portly, the less agile, and the lazy, that "it's not something you should plan or worry about. If your leg, torso, and shoulder muscles have the strength and agility to give you a big turn, you'll have a big turn. If not, you'll have to settle for a little less."

Hector Thomson, who was for so long the professional

at Machrihanish and the mentor of hundreds of youthful pupils whose parents, no doubt, palmed them off on him while they had their after-lunch siesta, put it in rather a different way to one little girl.

She returned after her third lesson and was asked, inevitably, how she had fared. "Very well, Daddy, but I didn't understand something Mr. Thomson kept telling me, and he said I was to practise it." "What did he say?" "Well, it sounded like 'Sweevel yir hinches'," and, because her father had a true ear, he was able to translate.

"Swivel your haunches" is not a bad injunction to someone to pivot, and whenever it comes into my mind I try to turn on the backswing, and the added distance on the drive is wonderful to behold.

Hickory Had Its Day (1970)

It is more than 40 years since steel shafts were legalized in Britain—the date was November, 1929—and within a very few years only a tiny minority of traditionalists clung to hickory and then usually only to a favourite club or two.

For example, I had a mashie niblick that remained in my bag long after all its companions, the putter always excepted, were steel-shafted. I clung to it because I thought—and still think—that you could put more "work" on the ball with hickory. It was kindlier, something to do with torque, and you could certainly lay it off and manufacture shots not possible with modern steel shafts and chunky heads.

Probably if I were compelled today to play with the hickory shafts of yesteryear I would cry, "Hold, enough," but at the time it seemed almost an act of apostasy to abandon hickory outright.

This is not to say I was a reluctant convert. Steel was legalised on, I think, a Friday. I bought my first steel-shafted club, a driver with a copper-finished plain tube shaft, that very day and played with it at Pollok on the Saturday.

The first stroke with the new implement was something to remember. I had a few practice swings, the club whistled through the air with a thrilling sound, and I had visions of drilling the ball miles down the fairway. Instead I topped the shot and the ball barely trickled off the tee. I did the same with my next drive, and the next, but happily the drive to the fourth was a beauty and I was off and running.

I mention this in some detail because it was the sort of

experience that anyone under 50 cannot possibly have endured. This is not to say that hickory was better than steel, or that those who played with hickory were the equals of the modern masters. But it would do any golfer of sensibility some good even to handle the kind of club that the great men of the 1920s had to play with. You can, if you are fortunate enough, do just that at St. Andrews, where the driver Bobby Jones used when he won the Open there in 1927 is on display. Or you can handle at St. Annes the mashie-iron with which he played his historic second shot to the seventeenth hole in the 1926 Open.

Both clubs are interesting in one important respect apart from their being hickory-shafted. The grip is uncommonly thin under the left hand—or perhaps it is just that the grip is the same diameter from top to bottom. But all modern clubs have the left-hand grip much thicker than the right-hand because we have been schooled down the years that we must hang on with the left hand, and it's easier to do that if you have something to hang on to.

The shafts of both clubs are very stiff, which is not altogether surprising because Jones hit the ball uncommonly hard despite his swing being so elegant and seemingly effortless. Both clubs would probably be considered today ill-balanced. I don't know what their swing weight is but I should be greatly surprised if they conformed with what is held to be standard weight today for players of power and quality. Yet it was with clubs like those that Jones won everything there was to win and with scores that were not very much inflated compared with those produced now. He did 285 in winning the Open at St. Andrews in 1927, and without the benefit of crowd control. Hickory had its day.

"One" (1971)

A pleasant tale I heard the other day was of a golfer who was driving to the eighth at Glasgow Gailes from the tee hard against the railway. He hit a fine shot and then jumped over the wall behind him—to recover his peg tee.

I have never heard of a golfer hitting his tee out of bounds, but the story sent me searching for a relic given to me last summer by someone who had been clearing the proverbial attic. It was a packet of the Original Reddy tees that appeared on the golfing scene in the 1920s and that have in their own way transformed the game. The American patent was taken out in May, 1924, and the British patent a year later—and I wonder if everyone who has made peg tees since realises that the device was patented.

The Reddy tee was so much of a novelty in the 1920s that the manufacturers thought fit to set out 12 reasons why golfers should use it. First, it offered "less resistance—lengthens drive." Then, "no sand on hands or grips," which was a real boon.

3. Invisible tee—no mental hazard.
4. Tee to height you like best.
5. Sanitary—no sand box required.
6. Clean hands—clean clothes.
7. No lost time—always ready.
8. Outlasts a ball—can't be lost.
9. No wet sand to chap hands.
10. Keeps sand off green (sic).
11. Great service—small cost.
12. Improves good drive—makes good drive better.

Bliss was it in that dawn to be alive and selling Reddy tees. No. 4 was clearly a fallacy for the tee is only 1.4 in. long, a mere midget compared with today's tees and useless for modern deep-faced drivers. "Outlasts a ball—can't be lost" is just a joke, and as for "No lost time," I should hate to compute all the time that has been spent on the teeing grounds of the world's golf courses by players looking for their peg tees.

Still, the peg tee was a wonderful invention and present-day golf would be unthinkable without it. It is now made in plastic, of course, and is virtually indestructible, but the first plastic tees consisted of a head and a stalk which readily separated under even an ordinary blow.

I remember buying one of the earliest plastic tees at an Open championship at St. Andrews—in 1927, I think—and the salesman spun a fine line of talk about its virtues: you couldn't break it, you couldn't lose it, and how many did I want. He was a little taken aback when I took him at his word and said, "One," which seemed to me logical enough if perhaps parsimonious.

The Reddy was a beautifully made little tee, so small and neat that I almost believe No. 3 of the selling points—"Invisible, no mental hazard." But, by the same token, it was so small as almost to be invisible on any teeing ground where the grass was long, and unless you had hawk eyes and an acute sense of colour it was much more easily lost than selling point 8 would suggest.

I must take out my packet of original Reddy tees and try one for my next game in rememberance of a wonderful and innocent age of golf.

"Slow Guys Finish Last" (1972)

A true golfing tale I relish concerns three Americans who descended on Nairn a short time ago on the enthusiastic advice of Charlie Yates, who never fails on his biennial visits to Europe to squeeze in a few days at that delectable resort on the Moray Firth.

The Americans lost no time in pre-empting the company of my friend, a colorful resident of Nairn, whom I choose to call the Lion of the North because he is almost unbeatable on his own terrain. They fixed a game for 2:30 p.m. one glorious day, and the conversation on the first tee went something like this:

"I play off 16. Joe here is a solid 24, and Bill—well, Bill's not so hot." My friend blenched but, dutiful in the cause of Anglo-American solidarity, prepared to shepherd them round the links.

It was quite a safari. The Americans were on the beach, they were in the whins, they plowtered in the burns, and generally made life a misery for their cicerone, who, ball-searching, visited parts of the course that in a lifetime of playing there did not know existed.

The climax came when they were making their weary way up the last fairway, with the clubhouse clock showing 6:55. "Gee, fellas," said the Americans' spokesman, "have a look at that clock. This is the fastest round we've played in years." As Mr. Punch once put it, "Collapse of stout party."

Americans have made many notable contributions to golf but one that we could well do without, as it seems to this rock-ribbed traditionalist, is their habit of taking an unconscionable time to play a round.

For this their climate is in part to blame. In high summer it is almost a penance to play golf. The heat is so intense, and the humidity so high, that one is forced into strolling instead of walking briskly. Hands have to be dried, there must be time out for refreshment at the ninth, and, of course, every putt has to be holed, every stroke recorded, such is their passion for competition and side-stakes. As a result, where we take something under three hours for a round, they count themselves speedy if they make the circuit in less than five.

It was not ever thus. The American climate has not changed but the habits of American players have. Hagen and Jones were not slow players, and they were tolerably good at the game. Gene Sarazen wasn't built like a grey-hound, but he covered the links at impressive speed, and with impressively low scores.

The modern generation of American professionals take altogether too long to complete a round. There are notable exceptions. Casper, for example, is a model of celerity and accomplishment. He is generally accepted as being the best putter now playing, yet he takes less time on the green than almost anyone else.

If slow play were confined to the gladiators, it could be excused on the grounds that they now play for such vast sums that they cannot afford to make the slightest error that might be put down to lack of care. Thus the touring professionals today never strike a putt without first lifting their ball to make sure that it is clean and, presumably, not lying in a hole. They then putt to within a foot and, bless my soul, up comes the ball again to be scrutinised, or handed to the caddie for unnecessary cleaning, and then replaced for the tap-in. No doubt it is a drill, but what a tiresome drill it is. The trouble is that lesser mortals seem to think they must do the same.

A Little Touch of Nicklaus in the Night (1973)

Last summer at Muirfield, a few days before the Open championship won so improbably and yet inevitably by Lee Trevino, I was reminded of some words written about Freddie Tait, who played some of his best golf on the East Lothian links. Andrew Lang once wrote that the only complaint about Freddie he had ever heard was that he played the bagpipes late one night.

I was abed at a Christian hour in my hotel overlooking the tenth tee when I was wakened by the unmistakable sound of a golf ball being struck. I looked out of the window and there, believe it or not, was Jack Nicklaus playing pitch shots from a patch of lawn in complete darkness. Thank goodness Nicklaus, for all his love of Scotland, has never learned the bagpipes.

They were pitch shots with a difference. His club was festooned with lights, one on the back of the blade, one in the middle of the shaft, and a third on the grip just below his hands. He was engaged in an exercise for some inspired moviemaker, and I suppose there is somewhere a can of film which shows the lighted path of Nicklaus's wedge as he plays practice shots.

He is, of course, an assiduous practiser. He works harder at his game than any other player of his eminence, even harder than Player because, I think, he works more intelligently. In the film of last year's Masters tournament at Augusta, which Nicklaus won from the word "Go," he is shown practising putting right into the gloaming after one round when his work on the green was awry.

Although Nicklaus is essentially a friendly, companionable creature who likes nothing better than a four-ball game in his run-up to a championship, he much prefers to go it alone once or twice during his preparation. He goes out with his caddie, plays round by himself, does his measurements, makes his annotations, and thus knows as much about the course after a couple of rounds as he could hope to learn in a week of less concentrated play.

Hogan was of the same breed. When he was preparing for the Open championship at Carnoustie just 20 years ago this year, he regularly played round by himself. He would drive three balls from each tee—one down the middle, one down the right side, and the third down the left side—to see which line offered the best road to the flag. That discipline, of course, postulates a command of one's game not given to many players and would be of no value at all to us frailer vessels, who have perhaps very vague notions of how to practise or whether indeed we should practise at all.

Macdonald Smith, who is probably only a name to the present generation but in his day was the most elegant of players and beyond doubt one of the greatest golfers never to win our Open or the Open of his adopted United States, had individual ideas about practice.

He always practised the shots he was playing best. In other words his practising was done to cultivate good habits rather than to correct bad ones. Now this appeals to my maverick mind. When we play a bad shot we immediately ask ourselves or our companions, "What did I do wrong?" How often, after we have played a good shot, do we ask, "What did I do right?" Maybe a little practice would tell us, and we might remember to our enduring benefit.

Bobby Jones, as might be expected, had some wise thoughts on practising. He believed in taking lessons and in practising the master's precepts, but he insisted that you must have a definite idea on which to work. "If you cannot think of some kink to iron out or some fault to correct," he said, "don't go out. And if there is some kink or a fault, as soon as it has been found and cured, stop immediately and don't take the risk of unearthing a new one or of exaggerating the cure until it becomes a blemish in itself. A man cannot do worse than practise simply because he has nothing else to do."

Jones is right, and when I find myself on an empty course and with an hour to spare, I play a game of make-believe for nine holes with two balls which I match one against the other.

Lighter and Farther (1973)

Sometimes of late I have been persuaded that I am doing a James Braid in reverse. He, as every golfing schoolboy knows, went to bed one night a short driver and woke up a long one. At least, that is the legend in brief. The truth is slightly different. Braid himself told the story thus:

"Something happened suddenly and in the most inexplicable manner, which I shall always regard as one of the most remarkable circumstances of my golfing career, if indeed it is not quite the most remarkable. Without any alteration of my stance, or grip, or swing, or any conscious effort of any sort on my part, I suddenly within a week was exalted from being a short driver into a really long one.

"How it came about was a mystery to everyone, including myself. All I or anyone else knew was that, whereas one week all my opponents were outdriving me by a good 20 yards every time, the next week I was outdriving them by the same distance; and the best of it was that this sudden display of form was not merely temporary, as all golfers know such things so frequently are. I kept on getting in my long drives, and I have no serious fault to find with my tee shots since that time, when I was about 17."

Oh, fortunate Braid! It was once suggested to me by a wise man that there was probably a rational explanation for Braid's being exalted into the ranks of the long hitters. He must have acquired a new driver which suited him perfectly, just as the great Scottish amateur, David Blair, once picked up a driver, in a sporting goods store in Chicago, which transformed him from a good, steady driver into a very long hitter indeed.

Blair attributed it all to the club, for at the time he had reached that second golfing age when he was at the peak of his physical powers and his play, though uniformly admirable, had remained basically unchanged for some years.

Ever since Blair told me of that experience, I have been looking for that magic wand that will, in my case, hold back the march of time. I can hardly hope to be as fortunate as a schoolmaster I met recently who was in a seventh heaven of golfing delight. An understanding wife had given him a present of a new set of woods to mark a special occasion; he chose them himself, naturally, and opted for a set half an ounce lighter than his old ones. And, *mirabile dictu*, what had started by being a concession to advancing years produced something like a miracle—he put 20 yards on his drives and, like Braid, has kept on getting his long drives.

Maybe, before I break the bank in search of a new light driver, I should resort to the old trick of heating the ball before playing. I know one man who always runs the hot-water tap over the ball just before he takes off for the first tee, and he uses a different ball at alternate holes, so that he is always driving with a ball warmed to at least body heat. And he swears the system works.

Playing By Guesswork (1973)

One of my boyhood heroes was Harry Wharton. He was not a golf professional; he was the pride of Greyfriars School, whose chronicles appeared each week in the "Magnet."

Harry, I suppose, was by modern standards an insufferable prig, a True-Blue Harold of awesome rectitude, but to devoted readers of his adventures he was the nonpareil. One of his adventures was so near to ending in tragedy for our hero that it was almost unbearable to read.

He was not rich (a point of identification) and to get to university he had to win a scholarship. He did well in the written papers and was quietly confident, as they say, about the oral—or *viva voce*, as the classicists would have it.

But he had reckoned without the Bounder, Vernon Smyth, the villain of Greyfriars. Smyth knew that Harry had a nervous habit of twiddling a button on his (Eton) jacket when perplexed, and, of course, he cut off the button unbeknown to our hero.

Poor Harry, standing before the examiners, was asked a tricky question, his fingers sought the comforting button—he was lost and so was the scholarship.

Something of the same sort happened to Johnny Miller, the new golden boy of American professional golf, during the U.S. Open championship which he won so spectacularly a few months ago with an incredible final round of 63, although in his case there was no unspeakable cad to do the dirty on him. He was nearly his own executioner. Here is what happened.

"I was really down after the third round," Miller has recorded, "because I had done a dumb thing. I had left the scorecard with my distances in my other pants, which were in my room. Talk about stupidity! The biggest tournament in the world, and I don't even double-check. I tried to play by guesswork Saturday, not knowing if I was 150 or 160 yards from the flag. I was just groping and making bogeys." He took a five-over-par 76.

One would have thought that Miller, not knowing whether he was 150 or 160 yards from the flag, would, in the classic phrase, split the difference. At worst, if he hit the shot exactly right, he would be only five yards from the flag. That would be good enough for most folk, but apparently not for the Millers of this golfing world.

Miller is not alone. Weiskopf at Troon during an interview after one of his rounds in the Open championship was seeking to explain how he dropped a stroke at one hole. In the course of his explanation he mentioned, just in the passing, "I hit my wedge 98 yards,"and the verb "hit" was used in the present, not the past, tense.

I find this almost terrifying in its implications. I have not the faintest idea how far I normally hit my wedge or my No. 9 iron or, indeed, any of my pitching clubs. But Weiskopf and the other modern masters doubtless know to a yard how far they can hit each of their clubs, presumably in still air.

That is why they chart the course and measure it every inch of the way—and they expect their caddie to be equally knowledgeable. At Turnberry last week I overheard one caddie say to his player, "It's 127 yards to the flag."

Certainly we saw Weiskopf and others do their little sums at the fifteenth tee on the final day when the hole was shortened by some 40 yards to make an allowance for the south-west wind which did not blow. Instead it whistled out of the north-west and made a nonsense of the ameliorative hole-shortening. Weiskopf trotted to the back tee, stepped out the concession, subtracted the distance he had stepped, and simple arithmetic left him with a shot of 174 instead of 215 yards. Mathematics for the millionaire golfer indeed.

It is all a far cry from the days of one of the grand old men of American golf, Walter J. Travis, who had the effrontery (as British golfers of the time thought) to win our Amateur championship at Sandwich in 1904. They blamed his success on his use of the Schenectady putter, a centre-shafted mallet-like implement that might have been good for breaking coals with, and promptly banned it.

But Travis had much more than an educated putter going for him. He had wonderful eyesight and was a superb judge of distance. Once when helping to survey land for laying out a course he was asked how far he thought it was to a certain tree. He estimated the distance to be between 155 and 157 yards. "Why not say between 155 and 160 yards, Walter?" he was asked. "It isn't," Travis answered, "it's between 155 and 157". He hadn't meant to be dogmatic, but he seemed so sure of his estimate that his companions decided to measure the distance and see how close he actually was. He was a little off. The tree was 157½ yards away.

Would Nicklaus, I wonder, or Miller or Weiskopf be able to guesstimate distance to a yard without the aid of their annotated card? I think Hogan might have been able to do it, or Bobby Jones, of whom it was said that his eye-sight was so acute that he could recognise a man a mile away, not by his general appearance and posture but by his actual lineaments.

When Hogan was preparing for his assault on the Open championship at Carnoustie, he set out to learn the course with characteristic thoroughness. He usually played by himself, and at most holes he would hit many different shots to discover which route offered the best line to the flag. After dinner each night he walked over the course—backwards from green to tee so that he could have a clear picture of the undulations and the general lie of the land. And, as the records show, the preparation paid off.

Let it not be thought that this crusty old traditionalist sniffs at the modern fashion of charting the course and annotating distances to the flag from known landmarks. I think it is overdone and that strokes are dropped less from lack of knowledge of how far the ball should be hit than from human frailty.

The Lord preserve us from the day when the golf professors have to use the higher mathematics to calculate the slope on a 20-footer, but I imagine that day is coming.

The Least Costly Hole-in-One (1974)

It was one of my ambitions when I played tournament golf to play a round, or a hole, even one shot that would get into the record books. Alas, there were no such golden moments, nor indeed, was I the victim of any such performance by an opponent.

There was only one stroke that might be an exception, for the man who played it against me was sufficiently proud of it to recall it in print many years later in an American publication then running a series by well-known players on their memorable shots.

In the Amateur championship at Sandwich in 1929, I met a fine American golfer, John W. Dawson, in a fairly advanced round. I had him on the hip, as I thought, when I was two up at the turn and comfortably home in two at the tenth hole while he was in terrible trouble on a sandy path so far below the plateau green that he could not see the flag. His caddie hoisted the stick at arm's length, and Dawson then hoisted his recovery shot into the hole from all of 30 yards. Collapse of your correspondent.

Even my two holes-in-one (which is twice as many as were achieved by Harry Vardon and Walter Hagen, who were not bad players in their time) were accomplished in the decent obscurity of friendly games. One of them, my first, was at the seventh hole at Portpatrick during the Munich crisis when the course and hotel were deserted and my opponent was a teetotaller, so my first "ace" was ludicrously inexpensive. (I am certain that my readers have no need to be told that the thrill of making a hole-in-one can be somewhat lessened by the old tradition whereby the lucky man must stand free drinks for all the golfers present at the club.) Thankfully I have been spared a hole-in-one on a crowded medal day, and I am quite content that this should be so, even though it might rate a line among the 20 or so pages in the Golfer's Handbook of hole-in-one incidents round the world.

But have you, the reader, ever *tried* to hole in one? To be sure, everyone tries at a short hole to put his ball as near the hole as possible, but have you ever tried positively to put it in the hole?

I did, once—try, I mean. I was playing with two companions at Killermont and first one and then the other put his tee shot to the eleventh hole seemingly stone dead. All of us were members of the 2 Club (where you must pay whoever scores a two), so I said, not entirely in jest, "I'll have to hole this if I'm to save two shillings," those being pre-decimal days. Believe it if you will, my ball touched the hole and lay a few inches away. My relief was increased when the other balls, as it turned out, were a few feet away and both players obligingly missed.

Two Free Sets of Clubs (1976)

An Edinburgh banker who is involved in good works as well as in good banking (and rather less good golf) is a member of a committee of visitors concerned with the rehabilitation of prisoners. At Saughton he was establishing rapport with a prisoner, and in the course of the conversation mentioned that he was an ardent golfer and a member of a well-known Edinburgh club. "Do you play much?" said the prisoner, who had something of a reputation as a recidivist. "Quite often," said the golfing banker, "but I haven't played much recently."

And then, rather apologetically in view of the circumstances, he explained: "My clubs were stolen from the clubhouse." The prisoner's eyes lit up—"That's what I'm in here for—nicking golf clubs."

He went on to inquire what kind of clubs his visitor had lost, and when he was given the name of the maker added: "No, I never took a set like that." And then he took the breath away from the banker. "I'll be out of here soon. Give me your name and address, and I'll get you a better set than you lost."

This story reminded me of something quite similar that happened to me. One of the least-known American challengers for our national amateur title was William Mandel, who played out of Split Rock. He was a stocky little man who earned his living as a trampolinist, and he was so good at his craft that he appeared in the Royal Variety Show.

He was an enthusiastic golfer of more than modest competence, and when he was selected for the Command Performance in 1933 he decided to make the best use of his visit to Britain by playing in the Amateur championship at Hoylake. He did not survive long in the tournament, but Billy Mandel made a great impression on those of us Scots who were staying in the same hotel. He had the engaging but disturbing habit of abandoning his share of a smoke-room conversation by standing on his head against a wall for 10 minutes. "Good for the neck muscles," he insisted, "You should try it." We didn't.

He was the first man I ever saw with a sand wedge, which had been invented a few months earlier by Gene Sarazen, and with characteristic American generosity he promised to send one to myself and to two other Scots. The weeks and months passed and no sand wedges arrived to sharpen our bunker play—and then, out of the blue in September, came a parcel with the promised magic wands. Mandel had lost my address and found it only when he was showing a variety agent in Chicago the Royal Command Performance programme, into which he had tucked my card.

That was a splendid gesture, but better was to come. A few years later when he was doing his act for the Glasgow Empire, we renewed our acquaintance, and I took him to Western Gailes for a game on the Saturday of his week's visit. We had a splendid day, and as we parted on the concourse of St. Enoch Station, he hauled his clubs out of his bag, a complete set of irons and three woods, and handed them to me. "I'm not going to cart these all the way home. Have fun with them," and nothing I could say would make him change his mind.

I had at the time a perfectly good set of clubs which served me tolerably well, but you cannot look a gift set of golf clubs in the grip, as it were, so I gave them a turn, and a few weeks later, while the best of our West of Scotland amateurs were in America on Walker Cup business, I was rash enough to win the Glasgow championship with the trampolinist's clubs.

The Secret of Golf (1976)

An earnest civil servant, who had recently taken up golf, cornered me one evening to find out, after having paid due homage to my long experience, etc., the secret of the game. He seemed determined to apply himself with the relentless energy of the ineffable Vincent Jopp immortalised by P. G. Wodehouse.

Jopp, it will be remembered, was an iron-willed tycoon who took up golf in the month of May and reached the final of the American Amateur championship four months later by applying to the game the same methods he employed in cornering wheat or manipulating the money market. I do not suppose my civil servant will follow the same pattern, but he might do worse than take the advice given to Vincent Jopp by Sandy McHoots, the professional whom he had summoned from Scotland to give him lessons.

"What," Jopp asked McHoots at their first encounter, "is the most important thing to remember when playing golf?" "Keep your head still." "A simple task." "Na sae simple as it soonds." "Nonsense!" said Vincent Jopp, curtly, "If I decide to keep my head still, I shall keep it still. What next?" "Keep yer ee on the ba'." "It shall be attended to", and so on.

J. H. Taylor's great exploits were over well before Wodehouse published his golf stories, but Taylor was a spiritual Vincent Jopp if ever there was one. Taylor used to keep his head down so diligently and look at the ball so penetratingly that immediately after impact, and even before he looked up to see where his ball had gone, he would step forward with his right foot and stamp on the divot mark he made.

It was small wonder that Taylor won the second of his five Open championships at St. Andrews, for he pitched like a wizard on a course where until then it was an article of faith that only a master of the pitch-and-run could win.

Henry Cotton used to insist that the hands had it. They were everything. If your grip was wrong, your golf was wrong. He once told a candidate for assistantship with him to go out and practise hitting 4-iron shots holding the club with his left hand only. "When you can hit them 140 yards like that, come back and see me." The candidate never came back.

The same Henry Cotton, however, once said a wise thing to me which has come to mind several times recently. When he was at the peak of his considerable powers, he was beyond question the best driver of a ball in Britain, possibly in the world. He was so good a driver that during the last Open championship which he won, at Muirfield in 1948, so astute a judge as Raymond Oppenheimer told me it was impossible to say whether Cotton's drives had finished on the left side of the fairway or the right—he was always smack in the middle.

About that time I asked Cotton what he did when he wanted an extra long drive. "Do you hit harder?" "No." he said, "I just turn a little more."

"Hail, Gutta Percha!" (1977)

We are all experts nowadays, and that goes for the humble golfer as well as the high and the mighty.

Not long ago a woman player of the most modest attainments greeted her partner in a mixed foursome competition with this cautionary comment on the first tee: "I hope you're not going to use one of these high-compression balls. I can't do anything with them."

More than a half a century ago when I was still in short trousers, I watched the final of a local tournament at Millport between two players of contrasting styles and physiques. One was built like a bull and smashed at the ball with a forceful swing; the other was slim, elegant, and had a graceful swing with which he seemed merely to waft the ball away. Yet he was just as long as his stronger opponent because he was using a Patent Colonel ball, a great favourite at that time, which weighed only 27 pennyweights, and his opponent was using a 31-pennyweight Black Dot ball, the required food for golfing tigers of that era.

We have travelled a very long way since the versifier heralded the arrival of the guttie ball c. 1850, with the line "Hail, gutta percha, precious gum!" Many golf balls made now could well bear the label I saw recently attached to a pair of elegant (and expensive) ladies' shoes: "Man-made uppers, man-made soles." And we used to say "There's nothing like leather."

Oddly, the very first gutta ball, which revolutionised the game in the middle of last century just as decisively as the invention of the rubber-cored ball revolutionised it in the early years of this century, was made from an old boot.

The "precious gum" had been used for packing a marble statue of Vishnu sent from Singapore to one Dr. Paterson of St. Andrews University. The thrifty Paterson family used the material to sole and heel their boots, and one of the sons, an ardent golfer and student at the university, made a ball out of a boot sole that was falling off. He painted it white but it lasted only a few strokes. He persevered, passed on the idea to a brother who improved on it, and the rest was the history of golf until Haskell turned the world upside down, and Sandy Herd from the Northern Kingdom won the 1902 British Open with his new rubber-cored flyer.

The Gold Watches (1977)

A few days ago one of the BBC's more perceptive Scottish reporters, Kenneth Roy, took himself and a camera team to the ghost village of Glenbuck in eastern Ayrshire to evoke the sport of quoiting (not unlike American horseshoe throwing), and the men who in the early years of the century were masters of this recondite and difficult art.

The game is still played by a diminishing number, but half a century and more ago it was the great game and Glenbuck was its heart. Roy came across one ancient who recalled the brave days and the man who was the nonpareil, primus inter pares, the pick of the bunch. He was called Tom Bone, and the old admirer told how his skill was so great with the iron rings thrown 21 yards to circle a steel spike in the ground that Bone would place his own gold watch on top of the spike and then throw a perfect quoit.

In the early 1920s professional golf in Britian had to take account of an invader who was almost as formidable as the great Americans who were then starting to come over each year in search of our Open championship. The first succesful one was, of course, the Scottish-American, Jock Hutchison, who won the Open at St. Andrews in 1921 after a historic play-off with the amateur Roger Wethered which need never have taken place if Wethered, in the third round, had not had the ill luck to tread on his ball and thus sacrifice a fatal stroke.

The play-off might not have been necessary for another reason—if a young Australian, Joe Kirkwood, on his first visit to these islands, had not taken 79 in his final round against Hutchison's last round of 70 and Wethered's 71. Had Kirkwood brought in just a reasonably good score on the final round, that would really have turned the world of golf upside down.

Two years later Kirkwood was back for the Open, this time played at Troon, and once again a bad last round cost him victory. He was winning comfortably with only four holes to play. He had to par in for a 72 and a final aggregate of 292, three strokes below Havers's winning score of 295, but poor Kirkwood collapsed at the difficult fifteenth and the very long sixteenth and somehow contrived to take 22 strokes for the last four holes—two over 5's, six over par.

Yet this same Kirkwood was a man of immense skill and, in certain circumstances, of iron nerve. He was not only a superb player, he was the undisputed master of the trick shot, the forerunner of the late Paul Hahn, who made a fortune out of hitting excellent golf shots with a club whose "shaft" was a few feet of hosepipe. Kirkwood did not go in for such major eccentricities but he had a most engaging act which he put on between exhibition rounds.

He came to Lethamhill, where I was a junior member, with George Duncan and gave his display between rounds. He hit intentional hooks, he hit intentional slices, he topped full drives so expertly that the ball bounced straight up into his hand. He would then play what he called, truly enough, the most difficult shot in golf—the dead straight drive (and why did he not hit four of these at the last four holes at Troon?).

He was also reported to have driven a ball off the forehand of a brave volunteer who lay supine on the tee and allowed Kirkwood to tee a ball on a tiny tee of plasticine—but if he he did that at Lethamhill I can't recall it. If he did, he certainly did not duff the drive.

I do remember very clearly, however, that he drove a ball from the face of a pocket watch—and hit a beauty, a beauty of a drive, I mean. For all I know he may have been offered a gold watch as good as the one Tom Bone used to lay on top of the quoiter's spike.

Having got the watch, made his little tee of plasticine less than half an inch high, and teed the ball, Kirkwood then went into his standard and possibly predictable routine. We were less sophisticated in those days and laughed heartily, possibly nervously if you were the donor, when Kirkwood took a practice swing and raised a divot. He did it twice, and twice dug into the tee. But the moment of truth was perfect, so was the shot, and Kirkwood handed back the watch with all the grace in the world.

The Best Kind of Golf (1978)

Oddly, although the friendly four-ball can be so rewarding and is indeed the commonest form of golf played just because it is so agreeable, some of the best games I have had have arisen when holidays or other commitments have cut the line-up from four to two and we have had an old-fashioned match, man against man on handicap.

It is then that you have to accept the responsibility of being your own man, as the modern catch-phrase has it. You have no partner to be a crutch. You can't go blithely for a long putt because your partner has got the half and you charge your putt miles past the hole and try to tell yourself that you would have laid it dead if you had to.

One Saturday night a good many years ago, I met the late Tommy Reid, who was closely identified with Patrick Thistle, at a social function. We exchanged views about our golf and found ourselves united in misery. His golf was "terrible," mine was "deplorable." So we arranged to play on the morrow at Killermont, expecting the worst.

We played like Palmer and Nicklaus, had a wonderful match, and the result, on the last green, was of no importance at all. We would never, I am convinced, have played so well if we had been teamed with two others in a four-ball.

Nor is there anything so exciting as the hand-to-hand encounter. There is so much to savour—the reaction of one man when the other rifles a long iron to the heart of the green and he has to follow; the body-blow when a long putt goes in to snatch a half; the knife-thrust when a holeable putt is rammed home to clinch the match. Do

not, I beg you, imagine I use the descriptive phrase
loosely. When Joe Carr was playing Frank Stranahan in
the Walker Cup match at Birkdale, he played two perfect
shots to the second hole in the afternoon and only just
missed holing from five yards. He turned to me and confided, albeit a little ruefully, "I thought I was turning the
knife in him there, me boy."

Last year at Turnberry, Watson and Nicklaus played in
effect a match for the last 27 holes of the championship.
By the ninth hole in the third round, they had practically
cleared off all other opposition and were left to fight it out
by themselves. True, they were still playing a stroke competition, but they could see the whites of each other's eyes
all the livelong day. It was a match in a million.

There is one facet of match-play that invariably attracts
my attention. It is the psychology of "the two more"—
that is to say, the situation in which one player finds
himself playing, say, his fourth shot before his opponent
has played his third. The position is familiar enough. One
man hits a good drive and then pitches almost dead. His
opponent puts his second into trouble, and his third is
nowhere near the hole.

The odds are heavily on the man lying nearly dead, and
most people too readily accept the situation, including the
man about to play "the two more." But this fourth stroke,
I insist, is a vitally important stroke and well worth receiving all the care and concentration that can be applied.

Maybe you are a dead duck; maybe the other fellow will
knock in his short putt even if you do hole; but that short
putt will lengthen appreciably if you get in first. Besides,
you are keeping the pressure on your opponent, and that
is what counts.

Only the other day I was playing a man who hit three
pretty indifferent strokes to a long two-shotter and was
barely on the green, all of 20 yards from the hole. I, *mi-*

rabile dictu, had hit two good ones to 20ft. He holed his
long one, and I had to do a deal of grubbing about to get
down in two for a half on a sloping green.

Once, indeed, I played "the three more" in an International match at Sandwich against J. A. Stout, the Bridling-
ton dentist who hit the ball like a hydrogen bomb. It was
at the long fifteenth and I took five shots to reach the
green. He was just through in two, chipped back weakly
in three, and then I holed from 20 yards and he took three
puts to give me a half in 6. Thirty years later I met him
again at Gleneagles and his first word of greeting was, "I
still grudge you that half at the fifteenth at Sandwich."
And I did not blame him a bit.

Obituary for the Driver (1978)

The sports spectator prizes power beyond precision. It is small wonder, then, that while Aoki and Wadkins were displaying their expertise in sunny Surrey, the item of golfing news that captivated me in my rain-stricken Northern holiday fastness last week was a tiny paragraph setting out the achievement of a 20-year-old golfer from Galashiels, Robert Rutherford.

He won a long-driving competition organised by a magazine at the RAC Country Club, Epsom, where the late Jack McLean was once professional, with a drive of 295 yards five inches—a handsome stroke which becomes something more when, as was reported, it was accomplished into a strong headwind.

I don't know whether the organisers, like those who run track-and-field meetings, employed a wind gauge, but if the wind was really strong it must have been about 20 miles an hour. According to an American expert in golf ballistics, wind will increase or reduce the flight of a ball by approximately a yard and a half for every mile an hour of wind.

Young Rutherford may therefore have hit a drive that, in calm air, would have travelled another 30 yards, or something over 320 yards. That is some hitting.

Of course, there have been longer drives and longer drivers, but there can't have been many better performances by some one just out of his teens. And hard on the heels of this report I had a letter from a very knowledgeable friend in the United States, in which he sets out his fears about what he regards as the grave problem tournament golf in his country faces today.

"Because," he writes, "the United States Golf Associa-

tion let the ball get away from them and because manufacturers have been able to put more kick into the clubs,
the pros can now hit the ball 280 yards even when they do
not hit it well. As a result, only a few courses are long
enough and difficult enough to test them.

"By setting up very narrow fairways bordered with
very thick rough, the USGA can keep scores somewhat in
check in the Open, but the truth is that watching our
tournaments today is infinitely less enlightening and stir-
ring than it used to be. When the terrain is almost irrele-
vant, half the charm of the game is gone."

Of course, the pros hit the ball immense distances, too
far as it seems to me when they often use their driver only
half a dozen times in a round, preferring to keep the ball
in play with a 3 or 4 wood or even a big iron from the tee.

The drive is one of the classic, basic strokes in the game
but with the modern ball and, even more, the modern
clubs, it has become almost a luxury for the professionals.

For one professional, the cavalier Spaniard, Severiano
Ballesteros, it even became a feu de joie when in a tournament some time ago at The Belfry he hit a fantastic tee
shot onto a green which no one else thought of attempting and his excuse was that he was bored with his match
and sought to inject some adventitious interest into the
proceedings.

For most of us, of course, the driver is the club we use
more often than any other except the putter. We have to.
We need every inch we can conjure out of our swing and
our equipment. We are the people, not the professionals,
who buy carbon-fibre shafted clubs at vast expense, or
titanium-shafted ones that cost almost as much, in the
hope that we will add one cubit to our golfing stature.

I have tried it myself. For several weeks a few years ago,
I gave a carbon-shafted driver bag room and myself a
succession of heartaches. One drive would go like a
bomb; another, seemingly equally well hit, would drop,

in a manner of speaking, in front of my nose. I got the shaft replaced with a conventional steel shaft, and my sanity was restored.

Of the titanium shaft I have less knowledge. A friend tempted me to have a couple of shots with his club that had cost something over £40, and I whipped both drives round my neck across a couple fairways. Maybe if I had drilled a couple of beauties miles down the track I would have been tempted to reach for my cheque book, but I doubt it.

Still, I dearly love to see a long hitter in action, someone who is not afraid to let his swing take care of itself. The greatest hitter I ever saw was James Bruen, the Irish amateur, whose looping swing was entirely his own and who hit the ball farther through the air than anyone I have ever seen—Nicklaus, Weiskopf, and the fabulous Jimmy Thomson of the 1930s, included.

In the final of the only Amateur championship which he won, at Birkdale in 1946, Bruen hit two shots into a wind on the long par-5 fourteenth (today's mighty fifteenth) on a rain-sodden course, smack into the heart of the green.

He used his spoon for his second shot, and when I asked why he did not use his brassie, he replied, "It's cracked."

PART V

THE LAST COLUMN
(March 15, 1980)

"The Man Who Can Putt Is a Match for Anyone" (1980)

Who, pray, is Mick Peck? Who is Michael Brannan?

Well, Mike Peck is one of the longest drivers in American professional golf, and Michael Brannan is one of the straightest. But, when it comes to winning tournaments, they are virtually also-rans.

I cull this information from a fascinating study of the first four tournaments of the 1980 professional tour in the United States conducted by one Labron Harris, who has the double qualification of being an excellent golfer himself—he was the U.S. Amateur champion in 1962—and holder also of a master's degree in statistics from Oklahoma State University.

Harris played in the Walker Cup match at Turnberry in 1963 when he was still ploughing the field of "lies, damned lies, and statistics," and when he turned pro he was good enough to win the odd tournament. Now, however, he has put his first professional qualification to good account and has come up with a detailed examination of what exactly the tour professionals do when playing for a living.

One of the tournaments put through the Harris computer was the five-round Bob Hope Classic. The others were over the regulation 72 holes, so his study took in 17 rounds of tournament play, a sizable enough sample, one would imagine.

Over those 17 rounds Mr. Peck's average drive measured 274.5 yards, so he is quite a clouter. Michael Brannan hit nearly nine fairways out of 10 with his drives, his percentage being .871, which is wonderfully accurate even when allowance is made for the fact that some of the tour courses in America have generous fairways and are nothing like so tight as, say, a course prepared for the U.S. Open.

The race, however, is not always to the strong in golf, or even to the accurate. One other statistic produced by Harris was revealing. The man who hit most greens in the regulation figure was our old friend Jack Nicklaus, who averaged .833 per cent, which means that he hit more than eight greens out of 10 with the appropriate shot—on the green in one at short holes, in two at par 4 holes, and in three shots at the par 5s. He was followed in order of merit in this respect by John Mahaffey, Charles Coody, and Lou Graham, who are not unknown to golfing fame.

Nicklaus, too, had more birdies than anyone else at the par 4 holes—he averaged between four and five such birdies in each round—so he must have dropped an awful lot of strokes elsewhere because he has made a notably unimpressive start this year.

The true test, however, is provided by two other sets of figures, the lists of those who scored best and those who made most money. Tom Purtzer had the best scoring average of 69.62, and he was followed by Tom Watson, whom we all know, and the improbably named Waddy Stokes, who each averaged exactly 70 strokes a round for 17 rounds.

As for the money winners, the leader was Craig Stadler, and his only other claims to fame as measured by the rest of the statistics were that his average score was only slightly worse than Watson's and that he had 64 birdies spread over the 17 rounds, just four fewer than Larry Nelson's 68.

What, then, does this exercise in golfing measurement tell us that would be helpful to frailer vessels like you and me?

For one thing, you don't have to hit the ball a country mile to score well. You don't even need to get the ball on to the green in regulation figures. Lou Graham hit nine greens out of 10 in the Bob Hope Classic through four rounds and did not make the cut for the final stanza.

In fact, you don't even need to hit the fairway with your drive—and here I don't rely on Mr. Harris's figures. We all remember Ballesteros at Lytham in winning last year's Open championship. The fairways were for his playing partner to walk on while he dived into the rough after his ball.

And there is the classic case of Ben Hogan at Carnoustie in 1953 when at one hole, the fourth, I think, he deliberately drove into the rough each round because that line offered a better approach to the flag. Hogan, of course, could be a statistician's nightmare, and an honest Harris conceded that no computer could ever take into account that kind of play.

The one golden rule that emerges from the statistical survey is as old as golf itself—it's aye the putting, or, as Willie Park put it, "the man who can putt is a match for anyone."

The golfers who win are the ones who putt the best, and the professionals are good putters.

The mean average of putts on the tour was 29.8 per round. Ninety-eight pros averaged under 30 putts, and 170 out of 217 were under 31 putts. Whatever allowance we make for little chip shots and run-up shots that are really only elongated putts, these figures are very impressive.

Yet which of us, who can't drive 275 yards or hit nine fairways out of 10, could not conceivably perform just as well as the best pros on the green where you don't need great strength? But it's not so easy. Putting requires as much skill as a long, straight drive, and that's hard to come by.

Publisher's Note

I first met Sam McKinlay in September, 1988. It was a telephone meeting. I had just finished playing Carnoustie, and I thought I had enough time before dinner to call him and introduce myself. I was expecting the conversation to be brief and, to tell the truth, I was apprehensive. Scots can be friendly, of course—that is one of their national traits. They can also be alarmingly direct— another national trait—and many of them are resolutely jingoistic about their Kingdom. I was afraid of saying something about Scotland that Sam would find offensive. Some years ago I heard that an English journalist of some repute had made a list of the best courses in Scotland and had left Machrihanish off it. Sam was outraged and let it be known.

I also recalled a letter that Sam had sent me after The Classics of Golf had published Robert Browning's "A History of Golf," for which Sam wrote a superb Afterword. In that letter he pointed out two minor misprints. I read into his words that he was astounded that anyone could be so slipshod. During our phone conversation, that matter came up but in a much different way than I had expected: he apologized for having mentioned the errors but assumed that I was probably as uneasy about them as he would have been. As a matter of fact, our conversation turned out to be as pleasant as any I've ever had. Sam made me feel that it was he who had been looking forward to talking to me. It seemed quite admirable to him that my golfing friends and I made annual trips to Scotland to play the famous courses and some of the less celebrated ones. He thought that this showed exceptional intelligence on our part. He was eager to tell me about some fine Scottish courses that had generally been overlooked, such as Royal Aberdeen, for he thought our group would enjoy playing them on our next trip. (He described Royal Aberdeen's first nine holes with rare graphic skill and put them in the same class as those at St. Andrews.) We discussed Carnoustie and, although he knew every nook and cranny of the course, he made me feel that my remarks about it were interesting and original.

I quickly discovered that day that I had been chatting with a modest man who was interested in what other people had to say. Sam, as you already know, was an outstanding amateur golfer who had played many remarkable rounds at Carnoustie, aside from reaching the semi-finals there in the 1947 British Amateur, but there was never a hint of that in his comments or any allusion to his own golf. He simply spoke about the qualities of the course that he admired and described the holes he thought were particularly outstanding. He was amazed when I mentioned how many members of The Classics of Golf had written in to tell us how much they had enjoyed Sam's Afterword to "A History of Golf", and he has never accepted the fact that his columns to the Glasgow Herald *were good enough to be collected and published. He was thrilled that we have shared many of the same golfing heroes, especially Seve Ballesteros and Harry Vardon.*

Sam McKinlay is a man without poses of any kind, devoid of ingenuousness, incapable of dissembling, and unaware of his tremendous talents as a writer. All of life is real to him and important—the great and the small, the major and the minor. Our fifty-minute chat when I called him from Carnoustie was, as Bogart said to Raines in "Casablanca", the beginning of a beautiful friendship. I have since had the pleasure of visiting Sam at his home on recent trips to Great Britain. The better one gets to know Sam McKinlay, the clearer it becomes how exceptional a person he is.

Now, I have the pleasure of introducing Sam's oldest friend, Kenny Cameron.

Robert Macdonald

Afterword
by
K. M. Cameron

I first got to know Sam McKinlay in the 1940s when he and his wife Marian began to visit Nairn regularly on holiday. Previous to our meeting, I had, of course, heard of Sam. He had been in the forefront of Scottish amateur golf since the late 1920s. His record in the British Amateur championship indicates his quality as a golfer. In 1928 he reached the fourth round of the championship; in 1929, the fifth round; in 1932, the quarter-finals; and in 1947, the semi-finals. He was selected for the 1934 Walker Cup team and, as a Scottish Internationalist, represented his country on many occasions from 1929 to 1948.

I believe that a large part of Sam's golfing success was due to the exceptionally high standard of his iron play. He hit his medium and long irons as well as most professionals, and what he was fond of saying about crisp strikers— "they hit their shots like a shutting jacknife"—was as applicable to Sam. The fine quality of his play continued until he was well into his seventies, and even then he often equalled or beat his age in medal rounds over his beloved Glasgow Golf Club at Killermont, which was founded in 1787 and is the eighth oldest golf club in the world. You, the reader, are by now familiar with Killermont, since so many of Sam's stories take place there.

After graduating from the equivalent of an American high school, Sam went to Glasgow University in 1925, graduating in 1929 with first class honours in English. A Scottish education was and still is second to none. In 1929, he joined the Glasgow Herald, *Scotland's finest newspaper, as a junior Sub-Editor. He left the* Herald *twenty-four years later to become Editor of the* Herald's *associated paper, the Glasgow* Evening Times. *His weekly column, "Golf and Golfers", which was renamed "Scottish Golf and Golfers" for this volume, began to appear in the* Herald *in 1956 and continued until 1980. This series, which appeared only during the off-season, had a wide readership from the beginning. Practically everyone in Scotland who played golf, which was most of Scotland, read Sam's columns, and we all counted the days until the next one would appear. He was a friend of the great golf writer, Bernard Darwin, and, like Darwin, had a marvellous memory, a fluent and easy style, and a good sense of humor.*

I don't suppose there are too many Scots who don't believe that their home course is the finest in the land, always with the exception of St. Andrews. I know I feel that way about Nairn, and I believe that Sam, who became a country member, shares much of my enthusiasm. "Where else in Scotland," he once wrote of Nairn, "where else in the world is there a course where the line from the first tee is a mountain sixty miles away to the west? Where else can a player swing his eyes through 150 degrees and see a headland forty miles away? And in between the peak and the headland lies a vista of mountain and foothills, of seashore and estuary that is a rare refreshment and a solace to the player whose game has gone sour. That is the prospect before the golfer standing on the first tee at Nairn on a fine day. There is no more attractive first tee in all Scotland, and he would be a dullard indeed who failed to find inspiration thereon."

Sam and I had many memorable matches at Nairn, some of which are described in "Scottish Golf and Golfers". As a rule, we partnered each other in four-ball matches and, on one occasion, our opponents were not unknown to fame. One was my local friend, W.S.I. Whitelaw, now Viscount Whitelaw, a notable figure in British politics and a former Captain of the Cambridge University golf team. His partner was Charlie Yates from Atlanta, Georgia, an Honorary Life member at Nairn, British Amateur champion in 1938, and as tough a competitor as ever visited these shores. McKinlay and I had a better ball of 64 from the medal tees on a good golfing day with a stiffish breeze. We lost the match on the last green when Whitelaw holed from eight yards for a birdie four. He and Yates had a better ball of 63. Sam later wrote: "It was the best, most exciting and wholly enjoyable golf match I have ever taken part in. We may never see its like again."

Sam played in the annual Nairn Open tournament while on holiday in 1958. After 36 holes of medal play, he qualified in the scratch match-play section. He reached the final where he lost to a strong, strapping youth. Sam was a senior golfer by then and had had a long week of hard-slogging. His tee shots lost their straightness, and he found the seashore on four occasions. The headline in the sports section of next morning's Glasgow Herald read: "Holidaying Sam gets sand in his shoes".

Another memorable match, which Sam described in one of his columns, was the visit of three Americans who were hosted by yours truly. The handicaps were 16, 24, and Bill who was "not so hot". We teed off a little after 2 p.m. and finished with the clubhouse clock showing 6:55 p.m. "Gee, fellas," said the Americans' spokesman, "take a look at that clock. This is the fastest round we've played in years". Sam also loved and used the story of some eccentric Nairn members who, on crossing a bridge spanning a stream between Nairn's first and second holes, noticed a body in the water, continued on their round, recrossed the stream again while playing the seventeenth, and not until they had holed out on the eighteenth did they inform the club steward to call for the police.

One of my great delights, along with other fortunate

Nairn friends, was to sit with Sam at the 19th Hole and listen to him reminiscing. He was at his funniest when recalling old Scottish caddie stories. Certainly you remember the caddie who would get so angry with me that he would take out his dentures to scream his oaths more piercingly. This was George Callie, known as Cocky, who had eyes as keen as an eagle and who could club golfers quite brilliantly. I seldom questioned his judgement, but there was one occasion during a match when I rejected the 9-iron he offered. Cocky was correct, of course, but the wedge shot which I played rebounded from a wooden bridge onto the green close enough to win the hole. Cocky was far from amused by my outrageous luck and delivered a verdict unprintable here. On receiving a generous bonus on leaving the last green, he let his feelings be known again in case I had not received his message. Alas, he spent his money unwisely and had to be bailed out of jail on Sunday morning.

I recall one of Sam's moments of glory. The fifth hole at Nairn is a very tough par 4 of 378 yards, especially when a south-westerly is blowing. I remember the match when Sam remarked on the fifth tee that the green was out of range in two shots that day, and I agreed. However, after a long drive, he fired a superb 2-wood into the heart of the green. The look of sheer joy on his face is something I will remember all my life, and it's why, I think, it was so rewarding to be a friend of Sam's. He loved the game in such a pure, spontaneous way. I can only close with a traditional Scottish salutation: "Lang may his lum reek."

K. M. Cameron